keep on Climbing!

onward,
Leanne

In a rapidly changing world, leaders face new contexts and different options than were evident even a few years ago. Women business leaders face unique challenges, some of which are common and some of which are driven by the culture in which we live and work. Author Leanne Meyer brings her personal experience and global vantage point from teaching and consulting with hundreds of active business leaders. *Climbing the Spiral Staircase* provides fresh, data-based, and pragmatic advice to help women business leaders thrive.

Whether you are a business executive, an executive coach, or an executive on the rise, you will find solutions-based, practical insights you can use immediately for yourself or to help coach those around you.

−CAROLYN DOLEZAL
CEO, Committee of 200

Leanne has provided me guidance in multiple stages of my career, and this book is a wonderful resource for women who are navigating the ebbs and flows of their own professional journeys. Using both research and anecdotes, Leanne demonstrates how cultural and socioeconomic differences influence our career decisions and attitudes. But more importantly, she provides practical advice on how to recognize and reflect on the reality of circumstances and to build the skills for a successful career—*Climbing the Spiral Staircase* is like having your own professional coach literally at your fingertips!

−SUMMER CRAZE FOWLER
Chief information officer, Argo AI

Leanne's story exemplifies the unequivocal use of power related to principal while balancing a deep concern for humanity within the context of the people and situations that she is addressing.

Leanne models this balance in her chosen role as an academic leader for business students, the majority of whom are often younger white men. Providing these students a female figure of strength and leadership is essential to providing new paradigms.

Her experiences, rooted in international traditions, provide her a unique voice focusing on universal wisdom that is necessary to bring about greater equity for women and really for us all.

This book tells that story.

–JIM ROONEY
Author, A Different Way to Win: Dan Rooney's Story from the Super Bowl to the Rooney Rule

In *Climbing the Spiral Staircase*, Leanne Meyer provides practical and uplifting advice to all women in every stage of their careers and life. Navigating through the ups and downs of your career can be challenging, and Leanne provides strategic tips to help her readers excel. This book will reinforce to its readers, men and women alike, that you "own your career" and is sure to be a trusted resource for years to come.

–JULIE BECK
Chief financial officer, NOVA Chemicals

This book is a gift from Leanne Meyer to women navigating their careers. Interweaving her personal experiences, research, and knowledge from years of coaching female executives, *Climbing the Spiral Staircase* is loaded with insights and realities that influence our ability to make progress in our careers, providing a valuable resource for those seeking to lead and succeed in their profession. Benefiting women with self-reflection, inspirational stories, and simply knowing we are not alone on this journey.

—CINDY PEZZE

Former vice president and chief technology officer, Westinghouse

With a clear-eyed purpose to help women envisage a future where they are strong, confident, and able to share their wisdom with each other, Leanne Meyer's new book is your best friend and coach. Having walked the path of juggling motherhood and career across continents, Meyer's sane, timely, and very readable book is a generous companion to forearm women leaders as they successfully navigate critical stages in their career amid gender and power minefields.

—DR. MARIANNE CAMERER

The Nelson Mandela School of Public Governance, University of Cape Town

A must-read for any woman or anyone raising a daughter. These leadership lessons and strategies are not only spot on, they are critical to success in the workplace.

—MELISSA RANDALL

Head of talent, Siris Capital Group

This is the book I wish I had when I was early in my working life, when I didn't understand that a bigger career was possible or the roadblocks I'd have to hurdle because of my gender. Leanne's advice and stories are insightful, fresh and frank, and grounded in practice, not theory. I'll gift this book to every aspiring young woman in my life—and to every father who wants to support her.

–BETH MARCELLO
Director of women's business development, PNC Bank

In *Climbing the Spiral Staircase*, Leanne Meyer provides essential guidance to women who are aspiring to something better in their careers. No matter where you are in your professional work life, this book will help you think strategically about what's next. This is an empowering book, one that will coach you through the changes you'll need to make to become the leader you want to be.

–SUSAN PACKARD
Cocreator, CNBC, HGTV, Food Network

Too many talented, ambitious women advance quickly to managerial roles but then fail to make the leap into senior leadership. What happens? In *Climbing the Spiral Staircase*, Leanne Meyer explains this gap. But this book moves beyond a thoughtful discussion of the challenges women face in the workplace to offer specific, practical techniques readers can use to accelerate their career and achieve their professional goals.

–DR. CHRIS HOWARD
President, Robert Morris University

Embracing the message of this timely book won't just add value for your career; it will add value for your *life*!

Leanne Meyer nails the critical gaps between surviving career navigation as a woman and thriving through it. *Climbing the Spiral Staircase* will have you positively assessing your internal dialogue, your aspirations, and your impact. Best of all, it will have you racing into the world to make your own kind of leadership success.

—SELENA REZVANI
Author, Pushback: How Smart Women Ask—and Stand Up—for What They Want

Climbing the Spiral Staircase is a must-read for women—and men!—in the workforce. It sets a clear understanding of gender bias, societal frameworks, and how those translate into our work lives—and how we can overcome and change them.

After reading this book, I was filled with so much hope and excitement about where we are and what's to come for women in the workforce. Meyer discusses women's pioneering spirit in a way that makes you celebrate how far we've come and feel confident that we'll continue to change the status quo.

Throughout this book, you'll think "Yes! I've felt exactly like that" or "Yes! I've encountered that same bias in my life" or "Oh my gosh, it's not just me!" Meyer does a great job of writing about the common threads that are present in the lives of so many women through the course of their formative years and into their careers. It's a strong validation of female experience.

You will walk away from this book feeling empowered with actionable ideas to take with you as you move forward in your career. From knowing your worth, to better understanding the systems you are working within and the biases you're facing, and learning tactics for negotiating, I have found this book to be a reference guide that I've gone back to over and over to refresh my thinking and to reenergize.

–ERIN HUTCHINSON

Global CMO, Merkle

With *Climbing the Spiral Staircase*, Leanne Meyer provides a personal and forthright guide to help understand the impact of various cultures and realities of the workplace that impact career advancement for women throughout a leadership journey. This book serves as a guide on how to embrace the challenge and provides strategies to mitigate the risks that exist to achieve the success any leader desires.

–ELENI LUCIDO

Vice president and general manager, United States and Canada, MSA Safety, Inc.

Leanne Meyer brings her incredible experiences, global perspective, and sharp skill set to not only articulate inequities that women face, but she shares practical leadership strategies that apply both within and outside of the workplace. *Climbing the Spiral Staircase* is a book that can benefit everyone who reads it!

–EVAN FRAZIER

President and CEO, The Advanced Leadership Institute

Leanne uses her extensive background in women's leadership research and executive coaching to candidly share realities of barriers to rising as a female leader. I applaud her approach rooted in data and research as the basis for identifying the varied obstacles one may face, balanced by her clarity that not all women face the same challenges. Once she captures your attention on a particular barrier, she then shifts the energy directly to pragmatic tips and tools a leader can immediately apply to their own professional journey. I anticipate this book and the action-focused counsel within will become a powerful tool in leadership development programs.

–BETH CODNER
Chief people officer, Eat 'n Park Hospitality Group

I have known Leanne Meyer for many years and have admired her work in the field of leadership development, especially for women. In *Climbing the Spiral Staircase*, she shares a lifetime of expertise in helping leaders to succeed in their lives and in their careers. With actionable exercises, points to reflect upon, and numerous examples from her life and career, Leanne's book gives readers tools for navigating the modern workplace. Women can experience the workplace in a unique way, and this book gives us all a better understanding of the history and inherent biases of the workplace and how we can make organizations more equitable for all employees. While this book is especially relevant for women, there is also much for everyone to learn in order to be a better ally, coworker, partner, and parent to women in the workplace and outside of it.

–BRIAN T. OLSAVSKY
Chief financial officer and senior vice president, Amazon

Leanne Meyer offers an eye-opening study of how we, as women, define ourselves and our work experiences through the lens of family, culture, and experience. *Climbing the Spiral Staircase* is a must-read for any working woman who has asked herself, "Is it me? Why is this happening?" within the workplace. Working through Leanne's book was like attending the best work/life workshop—instructive, engaging, thought-provoking, frank, and ultimately very, very useful.

–ANDREA CLARK SMITH
Vice president and associate chief legal officer, UPMC

The challenges women face in the workplace are part of conversations now more than ever before, but these conversations have not collectively reached the level of transparency and honesty needed to truly address the root cause(s) of the problem. Through her stories and experiences, Leanne Meyer sheds light on these challenges and helps the reader focus on solutions. *Climbing the Spiral Staircase* is a must-read for women everywhere!

–JOSYMAR ACOSTA
General manager, Pratt & Whitney, Puerto Rico

Through research and storytelling, Leanne Meyer addresses the hopes, fears, and crucial dilemmas faced by women throughout their careers. This book offers coaching and professional development advice for women and corporate leaders.

–MARIA TAYLOR
Chief learning officer, United Airlines

Leanne's lifelong gift and passion for teaching is expertly illustrated in *Climbing the Spiral Staircase*. In the book, women's career aspirations, and paid work experiences and outcomes, are illustrated through accounts of relational, responsible, and constrained performativity. The manuscript is narrated like a conversation with a good and trusted friend—deeply human whilst seeing the forest for the trees. In an evidence-based network of topics, she explains the most important aspects of what we know about women and paid work. Through storytelling, Leanne Meyer's accounts of having been at the edge, and in the midst of untangling, trying out and moving on, helps us to find our way through longing, fear, despair, exhaustion, relief, joy, and contentment. Leanne's father is right: she knows herself. In sharing this precious capacity with us, she provides a steady rudder for us to discover our own life of purpose.

—DR. ANITA BOSCH

Research chair, Women at Work, University of Stellenbosch Business School, South Africa

CLIMBING THE SPIRAL STAIRCASE

LEANNE MEYER

CLIMBING THE SPIRAL STAIRCASE

HOW WOMEN CAN NAVIGATE THEIR
CAREERS AND ACCELERATE SUCCESS

ForbesBooks

Published by ForbesBooks, Charleston, South Carolina.
Member of Advantage Media Group.

ForbesBooks is a registered trademark, and the ForbesBooks colophon is a trademark of Forbes Media, LLC.

Printed in the United States of America.

10 9 8 7 6 5 4 3 2 1

ISBN: 978-1-95086-351-8
LCCN: 2021920315

Cover design by Megan Elger.
Layout design by Mary Hamilton.
Author photo by Kaela Speicher Photography.

Advantage Media Group is proud to be a part of the Tree Neutral® program. Tree Neutral offsets the number of trees consumed in the production and printing of this book by taking proactive steps such as planting trees in direct proportion to the number of trees used to print books. To learn more about Tree Neutral, please visit **www.treeneutral.com**.

Since 1917, Forbes has remained steadfast in its mission to serve as the defining voice of entrepreneurial capitalism. ForbesBooks, launched in 2016 through a partnership with Advantage Media Group, furthers that aim by helping business and thought leaders bring their stories, passion, and knowledge to the forefront in custom books. Opinions expressed by ForbesBooks authors are their own. To be considered for publication, please visit **www.forbesbooks.com**.

To my mother and her mother, whose legacy of confidence inspires me every day, and to strong women everywhere, who are modeling for all of us how to live and work with purpose and passion.

CONTENTS

RECLAIMING AND SUSTAINING AMBITION–THE PEP TALK

THE "ICKY," AWKWARD CONVERSATION

RECONCILING CULTURAL FACTORS

YOUR TURN

YOU OWN YOUR CAREER

ACKNOWLEDGMENTS

W hat a curious process this book-writing experience has been. What I assumed would be a life-giving and expansive journey left me feeling isolated, super self-conscious, and uncharacteristically insecure in many of my opinions. I fully experienced the discomfort of making a professional transition, and I needed to practice the behaviors and mindset I write about as integral to "embracing the neutral zone." From this spiraling inward place, I am and was most grateful for the thoughts, words, and feedback of Beth Marcello, Jenny Belardi, Jillian McCarthy, and Shelby Livengood as they reviewed drafts of this book and asked their questions and spoke their truths and shared their experiences, all of which affirmed the path I was taking and made the book richer. Thank you! And thank you to Elise van den Hoek for the title inspiration and to Heather Wagner and the Lauras (Grinstead and Rashley) for holding my hand through the process.

It was also a surprisingly nostalgic activity. Unbidden memories appeared from nowhere and everywhere to remind me of the remarkable women I have met along my path who have shared their stories and leadership journeys with me. My deep gratitude to my clients and to the women who have participated in our leadership academies and programs, to the spirit of M. J. Tocci and Elisabet Rodriguez, to

1

Angela Arrington and Sara Laschever, and to the women leaders of CMU—Dr. Linda Babcock and Dr. Laurie Weingart, in particular—who have held space and opened opportunities for so many of us.

Given how unsettling and discombobulating the process was, I was grateful each day to step away and ground myself in the daily leadership practices of the Accelerate team. Thank you to Professor Ron Placone, Laura Maxwell, Michelle Stoner, Matthew Stewart, and Jarred Lazear, who have taught me all I understand of how empathy truly is a leadership superpower.

I grew up with only brothers, married into a family of brothers, and bore only sons. And therefore it may not be surprising that, for a book on women's leadership development, I have a surprisingly large number of men to thank. Our sense of self as leader, our leadership identity, is defined, understood, and verified by the company we keep. And it is through this network of rich relationships in my extended family—with my father (who I love with all my soul) and my brothers (and their families) and my sons—that I feel affirmed, understood, and inspired to be the leader they see in me. I am also grateful to the memory of my early mentors and sponsors, Professor Barend Lessing and Professor Ian Bellis, who opened up a field of study to me that gave me my career. And to Jaco Boettger, for showing what it looked like to encourage agency in others.

And last but never least, to Chris, who makes all things possible and everything an adventure. Who gave me the boys, Christian and Josh, who inspire all that I do. Thank you. I think it is safe to say we are "giving it carrots."

FOREWORD

I believe in the possibility of positive, lasting change.

Positive change requires three things: recognizing what you need to change, being willing to put in the work to make that change and keep it, and then knowing how to do it.

I've been fortunate to spend much of my career coaching successful people who want to achieve more. They want to get better. It's one of the key markers of successful leaders—this desire to continue to improve what *is* and then focus on what *could be.*

But many achievement-oriented people are tripped up by the paradox that the very behaviors that initially were critical to their success can then hold them back from advancing to the next level.

This is especially true for women who face specific challenges as they seek to progress in their career. Women are often reluctant to claim credit for their achievements. They may be overly focused on their need to be perfect. They may be quick to critique themselves and reluctant to criticize others. They may wait to be recognized for their contributions instead of advocating for themselves. And women are often rewarded differently for their behaviors, making it even more challenging to identify which behaviors they need to change in order to move forward in their careers.

In this book, Leanne Meyer speaks directly to the challenges women face when they are ready to advance to a more senior role. As the former executive director of Carnegie Mellon's Accelerate Leadership Center and the current program director of the university's Women's Executive Leadership Academy, Leanne's work focuses on assisting leaders to navigate those critical inflection points where many have outgrown their professional identity and need to make a change. She guides women through the steps they need to take to identify what is important—their passion and their purpose—and then coaches them as they work to develop new skill sets and behaviors that support their goals. She understands the importance of helping successful women achieve positive, lasting change—and she recognizes what's necessary to overcome the obstacles that may hold them back.

In the pages of this book, you'll find the guidance and insights that have helped countless women accelerate their careers. Leanne's advice is pragmatic and research driven, sharing evidence-based strategies for advancement and immediately applicable executive coaching tips. She has created a road map guiding you through the transitions you could and *should* make to accelerate your career. She coaches you to change the behaviors that are holding you back, equipping you to navigate the steps toward a career centered in passion, in connection, and in visionary actions.

This book is a coaching guide for women who are stalling in their careers and don't know why. It's also for achievement-oriented women who are not where they want to be in their careers and want sound advice to move ahead more effectively.

As you read this book, you'll begin to identify the specific behaviors that may be preventing you from reaching your full potential. You'll understand that what worked for you early in your career may be the very thing you need to change to advance further. And you'll be encouraged to look ahead to what's next and take the steps that will lead you to that future to which you aspire.

Yes, positive change *is* possible. In this book, you'll find the tools you can use to create it for yourself.

–MARSHALL GOLDSMITH

Marshall Goldsmith is a two-time Thinkers50 "#1 Leadership Thinker in the World" and has been a "Top Ten Business Thinker" for eight consecutive years. He is a #1 New York Times *best-selling author of* Triggers, MOJO, *and* What Got You Here Won't Get You There.

RECLAIMING AND SUSTAINING AMBITION— THE PEP TALK

*We don't find ourselves in a blinding flash of insight, nor
do we change overnight. We learn by doing, and each
new experience is part answer and part question.*

—HERMINIA IBARRA

When I'm invited to facilitate leadership training for a group of female executives, I begin by asking these women to identify their "passion token." This token is an item that reflects and represents a passion they have, something that inspires or motivates them.

I want to begin this book with that same invitation to you. Think for a moment of what your passion token might be. It should be something through which you see yourself illuminated, alive and rich with meaning. It's an object that helps you remember and connect to the aspirations and imaginations of who you are when you are at your best. But it's not just a reflection of your past; it should also help you envisage a future where you are strong, confident, and able to share your wisdom with others.

I'm always fascinated by the stories sparked by these passion tokens. During the training sessions, corporate leaders share with strangers the histories behind a pair of running shoes, a religious artifact, a medal or prize. I've seen executives produce letters from loved ones, sailing navigation tools, artwork, photos of children, handbags, prized pieces of jewelry, and even a bedazzled calculator. Each token represents a dream, a goal.

So, what is your passion token?

Mine is my grandmother's wedding ring. My granny was loving and gregarious but also one tough broad. In those moments when I'm feeling scared, I draw on my memories of her spirit for strength.

She was not well educated, but with sheer chutzpah and single-mindedness, she built a remarkable life and a strong family. She was a true matriarch, managing several businesses, supporting my blind grandfather, navigating the dramas of being one of eleven siblings, overseeing the lives of her two daughters, and still having time to offer advice on the best way to pickle pork or prune roses.

When I was a little girl, lucky enough to spend the night at her house, we had a strict routine. First, I was expected to kneel next to the bed and say my prayers for as long a time as she felt was needed. Then she would cuddle with me in the dark and tell me stories of her mother, who had survived the Anglo-Boer War in our native South Africa, living in a burned-out corner of the family farmhouse, searching through the plundered fields for any corncobs left behind by British soldiers, and grinding those corncobs into a gruel to feed her children.

If my granny wasn't sharing stories from the family's past, she was sharing advice. This always took the form of a lecture—not a dialogue—on one of her favorite topics, such as the importance of faith for daily living or the oft-repeated "No man is worth a woman's tears."

I loved my granny, and her presence and stories instilled in me an awe of what it meant to be a woman born into our family. In some corners of patriarchal South Africa, women were viewed as somehow "less than," as if they held less value than the men around them, but there was no sense of this in my grandmother's stories. Her example was a birthright, a legacy of tremendous strength. She gave me a gift of potency that was somehow different from what I imagine it would have been if I was a boy, and she instilled a confidence in me that, as I moved forward as a woman, I would always be strong—that I would be better positioned to do, to cope, to find meaning.

When I consider a potential model of leadership for women, I think of my grandmother—a woman who never set foot in a corporate environment but who instinctively understood how to blend femininity and strength.

I think about how proud she would be of how women have excelled in the generations that followed hers.

And I think about how dismayed she would be at seeing competent, articulate women—women like her granddaughter and like the remarkable women in the leadership programs in which I work—second-guessing themselves and struggling with feelings of being overwhelmed and alone, reaching for tokens to keep themselves grounded and strong. She would be taken aback by the conversations between these women at different stages in their lives and careers, women in positions of corporate leadership and successful business owners talking about their profound sense of isolation, of not being understood, of feeling that their lives are out of control.

She would want to push back and point to who we already are and encourage us to continue to discover our potential instead of dismissing, discounting, and diminishing the very power, perspectives, and possibilities that we have in hand.

What I learned from my grandmother is that women who know their stories, who understand the continuity and constancy of their lives, instill confidence in others. These are the women who are viewed as leaders.

PIONEERING SPIRIT

Leadership arises through genuine participation in the spectrum of living, in being who you imagine yourself to be. Knowing what is meaningful is foundational to being a leader and to being an engaged person. Leadership is a way of living; it's a lived response.

> **Leadership is a way of living; it's a lived response.**

Think about the strong women in your life. Who comes immediately to mind? I'm confident that it's a woman who is actively engaged in her world. Strong women aren't those who are passively sitting around, waiting to meet the requirements of a situation. They are *doing*, often with passion and energy.

Women are pioneers. No matter their generation, the industry in which they are working, or their stage of career, women are navigating new landscapes, shaping their lives and their choices.

The business world is constantly evolving. There are always new risks, new opportunities, new challenges—and a need for the right tools to create a life that makes sense in this new terrain.

Regardless of your generation, you are inevitably making choices that are different from those that were available to other generations or even to your role models. My mother didn't make the choices I made. My granny ran a business out of financial necessity, out of need, rather than by choice.

You may be pioneering by being the first in your family to graduate from college, or to earn a graduate degree, or to own your own business. You may be the first female executive in your firm or the first to sit on a board.

It's not easy to navigate that new landscape. There are all kinds of obstacles you will face depending on your age, your race, your economic class, etc. And entwined within all of those challenges is the factor of gender. As you work forward in your career, you need to understand the terrain, keep your eyes open, and determine how best to reach your destination.

A CLEAR VIEW

My father was a doctor. As the oldest child (and the only girl), I wanted to be just like him—I wanted to be a doctor, too. By the time I was in high school, I was convinced that my future was in medicine. But one day, when I was talking about my plans to study medicine, my father laughed.

"Darling," he said, "you can't apply to medical school."

"Why not?" I asked.

"Because you've got a uterus," he said.

I asked him to explain.

"You're going to go to medical school," he said, "and you're going to take the place of a guy who would be there, and then you're going to qualify, and then you're just going to have babies and stay at home. Why would you do that? Why would you take someone else's place?"

Let's be clear: My father loved me and wanted the best for me (and quite honestly, he probably knew my true inclinations were not for medicine). But like so many in South Africa, he had complicated feelings about the challenges women face as they seek to build personal and professional lives of which they and their families and communities can be proud.

I share this story to demonstrate the clarity of vision I bring to any discussion of women in the workplace. In my experience, American women believe in a false sense of fairness. Because it's uncomfortable to talk about gender, to talk about the intersections of gender and race, about differences in the workplace, it's easy to forget that those differences exist and that things aren't all equal.

I don't forget. I know that it's not fair. Growing up as I did, I never questioned whether or not I was loved when my dad would say things like his comment about medical school or when my brothers would tell me that my position as the oldest child didn't matter because I was "only" a girl. I knew that I was a girl, I knew that I was fabulous, but I also knew that history has equipped me with a very clear view of the challenges gender poses to an ambitious and determined woman. And I think that clear view is critical.

I frequently meet women who are at the midpoint of their careers who encounter an obstacle in the workplace, one related to their gender, and they are surprised that gender is "still" an issue. They are shocked to discover that, even today, being a woman might be holding them back.

I think that there's a place for an honest, frank discussion of what those obstacles might be. I'm not interested in casting blame or making excuses. But I know that there's a time and a purpose for open conversations about gender issues in the workplace, not because I think women are great—I do!—and men are bad—I don't!—but because I think that the only way women can achieve their career goals is by a thorough, nonjudgmental appraisal of the challenges they face.

Workplaces are complex environments with many different personalities and relationships, and it's important to remember that company values on a page don't make a culture. We have all heard the many corporate statements of "At (company name), we believe …" but the "we" rarely includes everyone. Too often, there's an impulse to pretend that we are all the same, that unconscious bias doesn't exist, or to reduce the discussion to a "girlboss!" mantra that's misleading and fails to honor the myriad choices women want to make, personally and professionally.

The reality is that the working experience is not the same for men and women. Studies show that women start off their careers with more ambition than men, but after two years of work experience, aspiration and confidence levels plummet by as much as 60 percent.[1] Although more women than men are graduating from colleges and universities with degrees at every level, women tend not to constitute more than 17 to 20 percent of any senior leadership team across industries and countries.[2]

> **The reality is that the working experience is not the same for men and women.**

What women are struggling with is largely universal, no matter the nation, although how it appears may be a bit different, depending on whether you are working in Taiwan or Toronto. And I believe there is a call for us to share our experiences as we have the difficult conversations about gender, about the obstacles we've encountered. As we share the stories of the women who've inspired us and mentored us.

---

1   Julie Coffman and Bill Neuenfeldt, "Everyday Moments of Truth: Frontline Managers Are Key to Women's Career Aspirations," Bain & Company, June 17, 2014, www.bain.com/insights/everyday-moments-of-truth.

2   Coffman and Neuenfeldt, "Everyday Moments of Truth."

It's important to note that while research shows that all kinds of women face similar challenges throughout their careers, Black women, disabled women, queer women, and other women of color are disproportionately passed up for promotions and recognized for their contributions in comparison to their White coworkers, not to mention the fact that they experience a considerably higher level of microaggressions, isolation, and undermining of their authority on a daily basis.[3] While the focus of this book is gender, gender alone does not determine how women are developed and promoted but rather the intersection of gender, race, age and ability, and other sociopolitical factors. I recognize that your story, your career, and the choices you make are unique. I also recognize that I am speaking from the perspective of a cis, White, straight, nondisabled woman, bringing a particular set of experiences and context, along with my own biases, to the lessons I've learned in the workplace—and to the advice I'll share in this book.

We'll unpack these facts and talk more about bias and privilege as we dive deeper into speaking about gender. My intent is to bring my whole self to this conversation in an attempt to share what I've learned to help all women thrive in their workplaces. To that end, I'll be discussing differences between how men and women are socialized and how expectations for these genders play out in the workplace, recognizing that the real picture is much more complex and nuanced. Other facets of your identity will come to play in *your* workplace, affecting you differently across race, age, gender identity, sexual orientation, ability, and a myriad of other factors.

The conversations we'll have in this book aren't abstract or academic; they reflect real stories and real lives. It's critical to view

---

3   Lean In, *The State of Black Women in Corporate America*, August 13, 2020, https:// media.sgff.io/sgff_r1eHetbDYb/2020-08-13/1597343917539/Lean_In_-_State_of_ Black_Women_in_Corporate_America_Report_1.pdf.

your career as a marathon rather than as a sprint and to prepare for the rigors and demands of each different stage.

WHAT'S AHEAD

I want to help you figure things out. I want to help you navigate each stage of your career in a way that makes sense for your goals and your aspirations. I want you to recognize your sources of strength and to celebrate the differences that have brought you to this place in your life.

Earlier, I challenged you to identify a strong woman. It's important to remember that whomever you thought of didn't emerge as a fully formed leader. There were steps she took that offered key training and guidance.

My hope is that this book will offer that equipment and guidance. We'll engage in a frank conversation about the socialized differences between men and women when it comes to perspective and behavior. We'll discuss strategies you can use to leverage the qualities that represent your personal strengths, enabling you to engage in a leadership style that aligns with your values and serves your goals.

In the pages that follow, we'll examine unconscious bias and consider why women are often uncomfortable acknowledging that they've been treated unfairly. We'll address the impact of cultural factors as I share more of my experiences living and working in different parts of the globe. Because the heart of this book is you— your experiences and goals for your career—I'll encourage you to take a careful assessment of your career and begin to identify the obstacles that may be preventing you from achieving more or progressing further. This is a book designed for you, no matter where you are in your career, so we'll review three different transitions you may need to make to help you advance to the next level. Finally, I'll share specific coaching tips to help you develop a mindset and skill set designed to support optimal career growth.

My goal is for this book to be a resource you can turn to, again and again. My hope is that each chapter will provide insightful moments that will help you better understand where you are in your career today and identify the skills you'll want to build to advance further. As you read, know that you are understood—you are not alone in your experiences or frustrations. We can work together to identify what has held you back and address any obstacles that are preventing you from moving forward.

Most of all, I want this book to inspire you with fresh energy for your career. I've noticed that, whenever women come together at the meetings I facilitate or the discussions I lead, there's a unique and specific energy that's released.

You can harness that same energy by stepping back and taking time to reflect before pressing ahead. Each time you pause to consider "Why am I here? What's my purpose? What do I want to do?" and then, equipped with the knowledge that answers those questions, you return to your workplace or family to try something new, you've harnessed a bit of that energy. That movement in and out, in between reflection and action, generates strength and vigor.

I see career growth as both inner and outer work. By regularly defining and reflecting on what matters—on what's important to you—and then bringing those intentions to life in your everyday behaviors, you'll find it much easier to reclaim your energy and your ambition.

CHAPTER ONE

THE "ICKY," AWKWARD CONVERSATION

One of the criticisms I've faced over the years is that I'm not aggressive enough or assertive enough, or maybe somehow, because I'm empathetic, it means I'm weak. I totally rebel against that. I refuse to believe that you cannot be both compassionate and strong.

–JACINDA ARDERN

Are you a feminist?

Pause for a moment and think about your response to that question. How you answer—how you define feminism—says a lot about our world and how the core concepts of feminism have been impacted by political posturing.

For many women, feminism has become a label from another era, one that no longer seems to fit our contemporary goals and values. BIPOC, nonbinary, and gender nonconforming individuals may feel alienated by the concept of feminism or excluded by a movement that they view as lacking inclusion.

I do not pretend to have all of the answers. I proudly describe myself as a feminist because I firmly believe that men and women should have equal rights and equal opportunities. I've seen, again and again, the unique qualities that women bring to the workplace.

Regardless of the identity you claim, in this book I will encourage you to be proud of who you are, to choose without fear to do well in your life, and to expect to be treated equally in the workplace.

Conversations about gender can be uncomfortable, as can conversations about the intersection of race and gender and about equality. But in this chapter, we're going to have those uncomfortable conversations, examining the data and acknowledging the challenges that women face in their careers. I may not always get it right, but having these conversations is vital. I'm not afraid to talk about those challenges, and you shouldn't be either. It's important for you to view your working landscape honestly and to acknowledge things like unconscious bias, the motherhood penalty, and how men and women experience the workplace very differently.

Some of the data I'll share may be discouraging, but I'm not interested in spending too much time reflecting on the problem. I want us to work toward solutions. We're going to face the obstacles honestly, study the numbers, but then create strategies that you can use to change some of those numbers.

We all look forward to the time when workplaces are environments marked by equality. But until that happens, we'll focus on the real world and the real challenges and obstacles women face—and how to navigate them.

Michael Kimmel is a sociologist who specializes in gender studies. He uses a question for groups that I've adapted for my own leadership training. When I'm standing in front of a group of female executives or young aspiring business leaders, I'll ask them, "How many of you had a grandmother who worked outside the home for more than ten years?" Very few hands go up. Next, I'll ask, "How many of you had a mother who worked outside the home for more than ten years?" and more hands will go up. Then I'll ask, "How many of you plan to work outside the home for more than ten years?" and every (or nearly every) hand will be raised.

It's a clear illustration of how dramatically women's aspirations and life goals have shifted in a generation or two. The working world has had to adapt to this flow of women into the workplace, and that evolution is still being felt in nearly every workplace in the world. It's also important to note that, historically, different occupations and careers have been available for men and women. Gender norms (based on unconscious biases, stereotypes, and socialization) have led us to tag tasks as male or female, both in the workplace and in the home. There are "men jobs" and "women jobs." For example, there are so few men in nursing that we use the phrase "male nurse" to describe them. Regardless of the kinds of work earlier generations liked, or where their talents/aptitudes lay, certain jobs were deemed more appropriate for women and others for men. Women have more career options available to them today than they would have had in my granny's time, but there are still echoes of these historical biases, reflected in the diminishing numbers of women as you move up the corporate ladder.

During the COVID-19 pandemic, I led a workshop for a group of twenty-five female attorneys. These women have been identified as up-and-coming partners in their law firms, career focused and successful. But the shutdowns and social distancing mandated by the pandemic meant that they were all working from home.

These women were generally ambitious in our discussions and guarded about any display of emotion or vulnerability. But after spending one month working remotely from their homes, these top performers revealed that they were suddenly confronted with an array of domestic duties in addition to their professional responsibilities. Some were forced to juggle caring for young children with the demands of their work or homeschooling children whose schools had been closed by the pandemic. Others were challenged by the need to prepare more meals instead of relying on restaurants or delivery services. And for several members of the group, the greatest challenge was the reality of additional time dedicated to cleaning a home or apartment, loading and unloading a dishwasher, or simply spending many more hours with a partner at home.

"This isn't what I expected."

"I hate this."

"I'm no good at this."

Never have I heard women verbalize so strongly what they didn't like about domestic roles, the work and responsibilities that, two generations ago, women would have been expected to assume without complaint. Their comments were visceral and honest and came from a place of deep frustration.

They had worked hard to excel in their careers. They were proud of their accomplishments and felt deeply frustrated at the expectation that they would quickly pivot to assume a new set of responsibilities in addition to those they were juggling professionally. They were struggling, confronted for the first time by the reality that many less privileged women wrestle with each day. These domestic-facing requirements were fully at odds with how they understood themselves, personally and professionally.

Not every woman's experience is the same. We are all pioneers, as I said at the beginning of this book, navigating new landscapes as our lives change, as the world around us adapts to new challenges, and as our choices lead us in new directions. But there are vestiges of the old world still clinging to us as we push into the new, and those expectations can hold us back when we least expect it.

THE GENDER ISSUE

Before I go any further, I want to pause and acknowledge that, while I speak of gender as binary, our culture is increasingly recognizing a much more fluid spectrum of gender identities.

I frequently lead workshops and classes on leadership and negotiation, and I like to use an exercise inspired by gender expert Barbara Annis as part of our discussion of gender issues. I invite the students and participants to the front of the classroom if possible. I then ask them to look at the walls on either side of us and imagine that those walls represent a continuum. I point to the wall on the left and say, "On this wall belong all of the uber alpha males." Then I point to the wall on the right and say, "This wall is where all of the uber girly girls belong."

Next, I direct the class to consider how they would position themselves on this gender identity continuum, regardless of the sex they were assigned at birth. Gender identity—that internal sense of who you are—can line up differently from person to person. We can use gender expression as an external representation of that identity via behaviors and signals such as clothing, hair, movement, voice, and body.

So, where would you place yourself? Alpha male? Girly girl? Somewhere in between? Somewhere beyond?

What I love is that, each time I invite students to participate in this exercise, the results are similar. Nearly every female student positions herself closer to the masculine wall, and many of the male students put themselves in the middle.

It's a visible demonstration that gender is a continuum, and how we identify ourselves is impacted by a variety of factors far beyond physical characteristics. Regardless of how we understand ourselves, unconscious biases around sex and gender, stereotypes and socialization shape the water in which we swim. They impact how we view ourselves and what we will have to address to be successful.

I recognize that exercises like this have limitations. I acknowledge the wide fluctuations of the gender continuum—it is not a simple binary.

But if we want to have a frank and honest discussion designed to help us understand the unconscious biases at play around gender and how they could be affecting our careers, we need to talk in stereotypes. It's the only way to identify the biases and formulate a strategy, because unconscious assumptions and biases that affect a woman's career are based on stereotypes. Exercises like the one I've described illustrate that while gender is not binary, our society—and especially the corporate environment—still largely operates in this way.

To address and understand these stereotypes, and so that our conversation is informed by the reality of the corporate environment, I'll be speaking about gender in binary terms, not to offend or alienate, but because my goal in these pages is to present an honest reality of the workplace landscape as it exists today. It's a mistake for us to say that the working world or society at large is gender neutral, because it's not.

EQUAL AND DIFFERENT

When I lead gender discussions, I often ask participants, "When was the first time you became aware of your gender? When was the first time you realized that your gender was different from another gender?" To me, the stories are intriguing and meaningful. Men's experiences often involve sports. One man told me, "I played ice hockey with the girl down the street, and we played on the same team until there weren't changing room facilities for her in some of the venues. Then she couldn't play on our team anymore."

I invite you to pause for a moment and think about this question. When was the first time your gender entered your consciousness? What memory comes to the surface? What insight can you gain from that experience?

When we begin the process of acknowledging stereotypes and identifying differences, we bump into the awkward realization that equality doesn't mean that we are all the same. It's tempting to identify differences as either advantages or deficiencies rather than simply resting comfortably in the acknowledgment that differences exist. We have to work much harder to hold those two concepts in our head—we can be different and yet equal.

From the moment a child is born, those differences begin to manifest themselves, especially in the way infant girls and boys are treated. Nurses in a NICU will speak differently to female babies and male babies. Little girls are picked up more quickly, held more often, and praised for their appearance. Because boy babies must cry longer in order to get attention, they learn from an early age that they need to advocate for themselves—to speak up and be heard. In one study of eleven-month-old infants, researchers found that mothers overestimated their infant sons' crawling ability and underestimated that of their infant daughters, in contrast with testing that proved identical levels of performance.[4]

In their book *Women Don't Ask*, Linda Babcock and Sara Laschever share research that demonstrates that, by age six, children can assign a gender identity to a series of objects, including a lawn mower, an

---

4   Emily R. Mondschein, Karen E. Adolph, and Catherine S. Tamis-LeMonda, "Gender Bias in Mothers' Expectations about Infant Crawling," *Journal of Experimental Child Psychology* 77, no. 4 (2000): 304–16, https://doi.org/10.1006/jecp.2000.2597.

iron, a dishwasher, a trash can, an oven, and a grill.[5] Consistently, the children identified the dishwasher, iron, and oven as feminine and the lawn mower, trash can, and grill as masculine. The masculine objects were associated with outside actions or activities; the female objects were all domestic activities taking place indoors.

As a mom of two sons, I'm very familiar with the sounds of boys playing. That play is noisy and aggressive. There's a lot of trash talking and boasting and fighting about the rules. When girls play, you hear very different conversations. Even if they're playing the same game—a game of four square, for example—girls will praise someone else's shot, apologize if they've knocked an opponent out of the game, and take turns. Girls and boys are equally competitive, but they navigate the game very differently. When the competition gets heated, boys will try to push through to a conclusion, complain if they lose, and celebrate loudly if they win. If girls' game playing gets too emotional, they may end the game before it's over and decide to do something else, closing down the competition to preserve relationships.

It's important to recognize how these behaviors and thought processes are inculcated at an early stage to understand how they impact our thinking later. These fundamental differences in childhood competition echo when we are competing for opportunities and promotions in the workplace.

ASPIRATION GAP

When I talk about bias against women in the workplace, I often get pushback. Younger women in the beginning stages of their careers believe that those battles were fought (and won) by an earlier genera-

---

5 Linda Babcock and Sara Laschever, *Women Don't Ask: The High Cost of Avoiding Negotiation—and the Positive Strategies for Change* (New York: Bantam, 2007).

tion. Men complain that the balance has shifted so that we are now living and working in "the age of the woman" where women are given more and more opportunities, even (some men believe) coming at the expense of their male counterparts.

These beliefs are false.

Maybe you are wondering, "Why are we still having these conversations?"

I think it's helpful, whenever I receive pushback, to begin with a reality check. That reality comes from data.

In 2020, women made up 48 percent of the workforce and 38 percent of managerial/professional roles, but only 21 percent of senior leadership roles were held by women; only 8.1 percent of corporate board seats were occupied by women.[6] The numbers are even more dire for women of color, nonstraight women, and women with disabilities, all of whom face more barriers to advancement, get less support from managers, and receive less sponsorship than other groups of women in corporate America. Only 6 percent of corporate vice presidents in 2020 were women of color, and these women hold only 3 percent of C-suite positions.[7] LGBTQ+ women are more underrepresented than women generally in America's largest corporations. Just four openly LGBTQ+ CEOs head these corporations, only one of whom is female and none of whom is trans.[8]

The two-year marker is a particularly critical point for women in the workplace. A study by Bain & Company surveyed one thousand

---

6   McKinsey & Company and Lean In, *Women in the Workplace 2020*, accessed September 10, 2021, https://wiw-report.s3.amazonaws.com/Women_in_the_Workplace_2020.pdf.

7   McKinsey & Company and Lean In, *Women in the Workplace 2020*.

8   Diana Ellsworth, Ana Mendy, and Gavin Sullivan, "How the LGBTQ+ Community Fares in the Workplace," McKinsey & Company, June 23, 2020, www.mckinsey.com/featured-insights/diversity-and-inclusion/how-the-lgbtq-plus-community-fares-in-the-workplace.

men and women at different career levels and asked questions designed to measure their ambition and confidence. As new employees, 43 percent of the women had aspirations of advancing to senior management positions within their organization while 34 percent of their male peers had similar ambitions.[9]

These numbers show that, in fact, women start their careers more ambitiously than the men. They've benefited from positive messaging ("You go, girl!") and have been socialized to be highly competitive.

But two years later, the numbers are quite different. After twenty-four months, the same percentage of men aspired to senior leadership roles: 34 percent. But the number of women who aspired to senior management dropped to 16 percent, less than half of what it was two years earlier.[10]

It's important to look at those numbers and wonder what has happened. What took place during those twenty-four months to so dramatically impact these early-career women's confidence and ambition? What about their experience was different from that of their male peers?

The answer is that the landscape looks different for women. While it's popular to think that women have more opportunities than ever before, and that old biases and attitudes no longer exist, the data show that men and women experience the workplace very differently.

For every 100 women who are promoted, 130 men are promoted. From entry-level positions to senior management, men consistently report more meaningful, substantive weekly interactions with senior leaders. Women report fewer opportunities for significant participation in meetings and fewer challenging assign-

---

9   Coffman and Neuenfeldt, "Everyday Moments of Truth."

10   Coffman and Neuenfeldt, "Everyday Moments of Truth."

ments. They sense that their contributions are not valued in the same way as their male colleagues.[11]

There are also significant differences in networking opportunities. Men and women start their careers in a similar fashion, with similar access to networks. But as they progress, women slowly start having less access to the "boys club."

Women receive less feedback, often from a stereotypical fear that they will become emotional. When women do get feedback, it's very gendered. They're told that they're too bossy, aggressive, or intimidating instead of receiving specific feedback—the type that will support and sustain career growth—such as "In that meeting, you interrupted the client three times, preventing us from identifying the requirements. In the future, you need to use more open-ended questions."

Why is this happening? What is the underlying cause? One contributing factor is unconscious bias.

UNCONSCIOUS BIAS

No one has shaped my thinking on unconscious bias as much as bias and discrimination expert Peter Glick. Glick is a professor at Lawrence University and a senior scientist with the Neuroleadership Institute. His research focuses on understanding and overcoming biases and stereotyping, and he has written extensively on sexism and toxic organizational culture.

Glick has crafted a quiz to help us better understand bias. Pause for a moment and consider your answers to these questions:

---

11   McKinsey & Company and Lean In, *Women in the Workplace 2016*, accessed September 10, 2021, https://wiw-report.s3.amazonaws.com/Women_in_the_Workplace_2016.pdf.

- Which gender is more likeable and warmer?

- Which gender is more helpful, supportive, and nurturing?

- Which gender is more trustworthy and moral?

- Which gender is more arrogant and egotistical?

- Which gender is more aggressive and dangerous?

- Which gender is more selfish (more likely to pursue their own goals at others' expense)?

When you reflect on your answers to these questions, what can you learn about your own biases?

Let's take it a bit further with one more quiz:

- Which gender is more likely to be offered help on a technical task?

- Which gender is more likely to be treated gently, not harshly?

- Which gender is more likely to be asked to serve in a support role?

- Which gender is more likely to receive challenging assignments?

- Which gender is more likely to be promoted?

- Which gender is more likely to receive a higher salary?

Remember that the questions are not asking whether or not something *should* occur but instead which outcome is more likely. When you stop and reflect on your answers to these two sets of questions, you will likely see that you expect bias to occur frequently in the workplace.

Despite the talk of "girl power" and "the year of the woman," the data show that women are not as successful as they are depicted. Why? These deeply held biases offer an explanation. It can be uncomfortable to acknowledge your own biases. But the reality is that we all have them—unconscious and otherwise. Glick makes the case that some biases have become so ingrained within our culture that what was once perhaps unconscious morphs into a largely consciously held belief (e.g., that women should be "likeable" and that men should be respected). He states that these explicit biases are prescriptive in nature ("women *should* be likeable," "men *should* try to gain respect") and are often at the root of much of the challenges women face in their careers—in an effort to become likeable, she may lose respect; in effort to gain respect, she may be seen as unlikeable. Biases may be automatic, but discrimination is not inevitable.

I said it earlier, but it's a key point: Women experience a very different workplace than men. And because we experience a different environment, it affects how we act and perform in ways that can often be negative.

There are four areas that represent these central differences between how men and women experience their work environments: the double bind, M-shaped careers, career motivation, and leadership development. Let's spend a few minutes considering each of these four areas.

The *double bind* reflects the Goldilocks-like paradox that women are either too soft or too tough but never just right. The bar is set higher for women while the rewards are lower; they are asked to demonstrate leadership skills over and over again.

In this way, women are judged for what they aren't as much as for what they are. They are viewed, in a sense, like deficient men. If women demonstrate thoughtfulness or kindness, they are perceived as weak. If they are supportive of colleagues, they are judged as not being independent enough to be a leader. If they behave more aggressively, they are described as a bitch or a dragon lady.

What women learn is that they can be judged as competent or likeable but not both. The more successful they are, the less likeable they are perceived as being—by both men and women.[12]

> **What women learn is that they can be judged as competent or likeable but not both.**

Test your own biases here. If I asked you, "Name a woman who is very competent," who comes to mind? Now, what happens if I ask, "Do you like her?"

These unconscious biases play out clearly when an employee becomes a parent. It's the difference between what we call the "motherhood penalty" and the "fatherhood bonus." As soon as women start having children, we see a dip in their salaries. Employers assume that they've lost their ambition and that their focus has shifted. The same assumption is not true for men. In fact, when men become fathers, employers often say something like "This will help them get their act together" or "Now they're going to settle down and get serious about the future." There is a common perception that fatherhood will improve a man's ability to be successful, and their salaries often increase to reflect that belief.

My thinking on the *M-shaped career* has been shaped by the writing of Avivah Wittenberg-Cox. She identifies four phases of a woman's career, loosely representing the rises and falls of an "M." In their twenties, many women are ambitious—it's a time of learning, growth, and independence. In their thirties, women often see their careers stall, impacted by parenting and the realities of today's corporate culture. The forties, according to Wittenberg-Cox, are marked by reacceleration,

---

12   Catalyst, *The Double-Bind Dilemma for Women in Leadership: Damned if You Do, Doomed if You Don't*, accessed September 10 2021, www.catalyst.org/wp-content/uploads/2019/01/The_Double_Bind_Dilemma_for_Women_in_Leadership_Damned_if_You_Do_Doomed_if_You_Dont.pdf.

as women begin to refocus on career priorities using the foundations they built earlier. Finally, in their fifties, Wittenberg-Cox suggests that women will experience their peak career in a time of self-actualization, often sparked by children leaving home and the resulting empty nest.[13]

I'm fascinated by this idea of an M-shaped career based on ebbs and flows, and it's a concept that resonates with many women I know. Women often rise very quickly early in their careers before encountering a dip—a dip that may be caused by caring for children or elderly parents.

But I think there's something equally significant to consider in these dipping points. The first arc in a career is marked by achievement. You can be successful if you hit specific goals. But in the second arc of your career, the ability to build networks of influence becomes deeply important. And as we saw earlier, women experience bias when it comes to networking opportunities. They may not have the time to have lunch or go out for drinks with colleagues if they are juggling child- or eldercare. And an unexpected side effect of the important accomplishments of the #MeToo movement is that male managers are uncomfortable being alone with a female employee. There are fewer invitations to a breakfast or lunch meeting; if they are invited, a male employee is often invited as well. There are far fewer opportunities to build one-on-one connections and demonstrate competence.

It can be discouraging to acknowledge this gap, but I think it's helpful to remember that it is simply a dip, not an end point. Data show that women who continue to press ahead will experience success in their careers—the "M" will go back up again. But their rise will take place on average ten years later than that of their male colleagues.[13]

---

13   Avivah Wittenberg-Cox and Alison Maitland, *Why Women Mean Business: Under-standing the Emergence of Our Next Economic Revolution* (San Francisco: Jossey-Bass, 2008).

One study looked at female CEOs of Fortune 500 companies to identify the secret to their success.[14] Was it an MBA? Was it being a graduate of a prestigious school? Was it their specific area of specialization or unique work experience?

The answer was much simpler: longevity. These women had worked longer for their organizations. On average, male CEOs had spent fifteen years with their organization; the female CEOs had spent twenty-three years.

Unconscious bias is also revealed when we consider *career motivation*—what women want from their career. Both men and women are nearly equally ambitious when it comes to getting promoted to the next level, but distinct gaps emerge when both genders are asked about their desire to become a chief executive and their belief that this outcome is likely. Universities have dedicated significant resources to facilitating gender parity in areas of study once male dominated—areas like engineering or computer science—so it is no wonder that women begin their careers feeling qualified to be successful. On the other end of the spectrum, there has been substantial focus (and legislation) directed to creating greater gender equity in the boardroom.

Although both of these areas need consistent focus, a major gap of attention seems to be in the "messy middle," as we call it, where employees spend the most—and the most formative—years of their career, and it's here where we see women's confidence falling. And it's also here where unconscious biases flavor our everyday interactions. These are the experiences that will shape what we think we are capable of and whether the effort is worth it. Will our aspiration be fortified? Our confidence built or eroded? We need to pay attention, we need data to understand what

---

14   Sarah Dillard and Vanessa Lipschitz, "Research: How Female CEOs Actually Get to the Top," *Harvard Business Review*, November 6, 2014, https://hbr.org/2014/11/research-how-female-ceos-actually-get-to-the-top.

could be going on and not automatically assume we are not good at what we do, and we need strategies to mitigate what could be at play.

Finally, we come to *leadership development*. This is the focus of much of my work, and I'll spend time in this book partnering with you to help you foster the skills and capabilities that you'll need for leadership. It's not enough to take the same generic leadership training programs used for men and adopt an "add woman and stir" approach. Gender matters when it comes to developing leaders. For now, let's start with an acknowledgment that unconscious bias exists. This is simply a reality of the landscape. I'm not trying to offer any training to de-bias you or your workplace; I don't find those to be at all effective (and neither does the research). Instead, I want to encourage you to take a clear view of the landscape so that you'll be able to identify in advance potential obstacles to your career aspirations and begin to access the tools you'll need to overcome them.

> **Gender matters when it comes to developing leaders.**

Unconscious bias shapes how women are viewed in the workplace, so it's critical for you to firmly anchor your career identity in a sense of purpose. There will be times when you wonder, "Why am I doing this? Why do I have to put up with this rubbish?" At those times, you want to have a clear answer—a firm sense of your career goals and aspirations—to give energy to your efforts to move past a specific block or navigate through a career lull.

MOVING FORWARD

I understand. It can be discouraging to study the data, to identify the challenges and recognize that you'll have to fight harder and longer than your male peers to be successful.

My intent with this book is not to "fix" women so they adapt to a male workplace but rather to equip you with the skills that the data indicate can be missing in a woman's repertoire—things like negotiation skills, building networks of influence, visioning and inspiring change—to allow you to be successful no matter your environment. In this way, we can address the transition dilemma of that M-shaped curve and the sense that what may have worked early in your career may not help you navigate to the next level.

I'm not interested in just sharing data and then stepping back and admiring the problem. I want to share solutions, too.

In the next chapter, we'll examine some of the cultural factors that shape your ability to achieve career goals. We'll discuss the impact of familial and communal expectations and how they can affect your leadership development. I'll share some of the patterns of behavior I've seen in high-achieving women and reveal strategies that will help you reconcile your leadership aspirations with the pressures and expectations of your unique family and community background.

There is so much I want to share with you. Let's get started.

Reflection Points

1. Consider the language you use to describe boys and girls, men and women. Do your words reveal certain biases?

   _____

   _____

   _____

   _____

   _____

2. As a leader, are you more likely to support a man with consistently high workplace evaluations or a woman with equally high evaluations? Does your selection have anything to do with likeability?

   _____

   _____

   _____

   _____

   _____

3. In a mixed-gender meeting, observe how ideas are proposed, how credit is distributed, and when conversations are interrupted. Do you see evidence of gender bias in these interactions?

_____

_____

_____

_____

_____

CHAPTER TWO

RECONCILING CULTURAL FACTORS

How Cultural Identity and Public Policy
Shape Our Understanding of What's Possible

The antiquated rhetoric of "having it all" disregards the basis of
every economic relationship— the idea of trade-offs. All of us are
dealing with the constrained optimization that is life, attempting
to maximize our utility based on parameters like career, kids,
relationships, etc., doing our best to allocate the resource of time.
Due to the scarcity of this resource, therefore, none of us can
"have it all," and those who claim to are most likely lying.

–SHARON POCZTER

Until now, my focus in this book has been on encouraging you to identify yourself within the context of gender. It's important to recognize that workplaces are gendered environments and that those gendered environments will impact your ability to thrive and succeed.

But there's an understanding that I feel is equally important, and that's the impact of cultural factors. Where you come from not only shapes how you think about your career but also influences the choices you make about where and how you'll live, about whether you marry or commit to a partner. It impacts your decision whether or not to have children—and if so, when and how many.

> It's important to recognize that workplaces are gendered environments and that those gendered environments will impact your ability to thrive and succeed.

The purpose of this chapter is not to make judgments on the choices that you've made and will make in the future. Quite the opposite. It's to reflect the knowledge that cultural factors predispose us to certain attitudes and responses to each of those choices. You may be a mother. You may—because of choice or circumstance—not have children. I've been a partner, a wife, and a mother, so I will speak from those positions, not because I think that they are the "right" or better choices but simply because those reflect my own story. I've lived on three different continents and have experienced, both personally and professionally, the impact cultural identity and public policy have had on my own decision-making.

I do find it interesting that, even as I write this, I worry about speaking to you from a position of inclusivity, no matter your story or your culture or your choices. The quote from Sharon Poczter at the start of this chapter acknowledges that challenge. It's not possible to "have it all"—your time is finite, and your choice to pursue one path, be it investing in a career or relationship or parenting, likely comes at the expense of investing in another area.

So let's start with a question: What does it mean to be a good mother?

Don't read on too quickly. Pause for a moment and reflect on your response to that question. How you answer will be impacted by your family of origin, by your country's culture and its public policies. Consider how your own choices about parenting and your career may echo in your response to this question.

Because so many women are making decisions about parenting in the context of their careers, I want to spend a little time thinking about this question of trade-offs and how we define a "good" mother. The way you think about what it means to have a meaningful career, be a good mother, and live a life that makes you proud is deeply influenced by cultural understandings of each of these three elements. It's also a product of public policies. Finally, it's shaped by where you are in your career and life continuum—recall the M-shaped curve we discussed in the previous chapter.

Sociologist Caitlyn Collins examines how cultural factors shape our understanding of a "good mother" in her book *Making Motherhood Work*.[15] Collins demonstrates how social policies influence the ways in which we think about careers by considering the context of working women in the former East Germany. In Communist countries, work was mandated—for men and women. The concept of a "working mother" didn't carry the weight of guilt or the implication of choice that it does in America today. All women worked; if you were a mother, you were still expected to work outside the home. Some women in that culture may have curtailed their working hours, or their ambitions, but employment was mandated. It is worth noting that Angela Merkel, the first

---

15   Caitlyn Collins, *Making Motherhood Work: How Women Manage Careers and Caregiving* (Princeton, NJ: Princeton University Press, 2019).

female chancellor of Germany, grew up in the former East Germany.

Germany makes a useful illustration for this discussion because we can contrast the views of working mothers in East and West Germany before the country was reunified in 1990. In West Germany, a "good mother" was a mother who stayed at home to raise the children. Women were expected to work until they were pregnant, stay at home while their children were young—childcare was not available for children younger than three years old—and then resume working on a part-time basis when their children were older.

The reunified Germany of today has preserved the latter understanding of what it means to be a "good mother." One of the gravest insults that can be hurled at a working woman is to call her a *rabenmutter*—literally, a "raven mother." The implication is that a working woman is like a raven, abandoning her children in their nest. The results of this cultural pressure are clear: According to FidAR, a Berlin-based women's advocacy group, only one-third of all leadership positions in Germany are held by women, a figure that has remained stagnant for years.[16] A study by the Swedish-German Allbright Foundation found that the executive boards of 110 of Germany's 160 publicly traded companies have no female members at all—of 697 total members, only 56 are women.[17]

Social democratic states like Norway, Sweden, Denmark, and Finland come at this from a far more egalitarian perspective. Their social systems are built on a foundation that assumes that mothers should be able to work. These countries offer parental leave, rather than maternity

---

16   Diana Hodali, "Germany Needs More Women in Leadership Positions," DW.com, November 10, 2018, www.dw.com/en/germany-needs-more-women-in-leadership-positions/a-45853079.

17   "Female Representation Lagging on German Public Boards," DW.com, February 8, 2018, www.dw.com/en/female-representation-lagging-on-german-public-boards/a-44921630.

leave, underscoring the attitude that parenting is a shared responsibility. Parental leave lasts for one year—for both partners—and there is universal childcare available when parents are ready to resume their working careers. In these more egalitarian cultural contexts, public policies support the ability of both men and women to participate in breadwinning and caregiving. And the concept of "stay-at-home mother" is nonexistent; the assumption is that women and men will work, whether or not they choose to have children.

When it comes to gender equality, countries such as Finland, Norway, and Sweden are global leaders. That list also includes Iceland and Rwanda. Rwanda has one of the highest rates of female labor participation in the world at 86 percent. While there are enormous disparities between Rwanda and these other industrialized countries (including in terms of life expectancy and income but in particular as it relates to the Rwandan Civil War—the male population was depleted so considerably in the conflict that more women began to occupy professional positions), in the US, that figure stands at 56 percent—and is declining. In Rwanda, women earn 88 cents for every dollar men do; in the US, it's 74 cents.[18]

We can also consider Japan, which—over the past two decades—has introduced one of the most generous parental leave benefits in the world and has approved workstyle reforms that mandate overtime limits and equal pay for equal work. As a result, Japan has seen its female labor participation ratio surge from 56 percent to 71 percent, surpassing that of the US and Europe.[19]

---

18   Stéphanie Thomson, "How Rwanda Beats the United States and France in Gender Equality," World Economic Forum, May 2, 2017, www.weforum.org/agenda/2017/05/how-rwanda-beats-almost-every-other-country-in-gender-equality.

19   Kathy Matsui, Hiromi Suzuki, and Kazunori Tatebe, "20 Years on Womenomics 5.0: Progress, Areas for Improvement, Potential 15% GDP Boost," Goldman Sachs, April 18, 2019, www.goldmansachs.com/insights/pages/womenomics-5.0/multimedia/womenomics-5.0-report.pdf.

This is why it's important to consider cultural factors in our discussion of women shaping meaningful careers. In countries where there is significant public support for women to return to work after having children, women are far less conflicted in their understanding of what it means to be a "good mother" than in countries like Germany or Italy—or the United States.

In America, women are expected to figure things out on their own. We value the idea of individual choice, of personal freedom and personal responsibility, but we also must recognize the cost of this individualistic attitude on women's careers. In the United States, companies are not required to offer paid parental leave. There is no universal childcare, nor is there universal healthcare. The US has the highest gender wage gap in the developed world, no minimum standard for vacation and sick days, and shockingly high maternal and child poverty rates. There are no public policies that support women who choose to or need to work while having children; instead, this country is marked by some of the most inflexible workplaces in the developed world. The US is one of just eight countries with no national policy mandating paid maternity leave for workers. To date, only three US states (California, New York, and Rhode Island) have implemented paid family leave programs, and five states (California, Hawaii, New Jersey, New York, and Rhode Island) guarantee workers' access to paid temporary disability leave. Absent a federal paid family leave policy, it is primarily employers who determine whether employees have access to paid time off to care for a new child or an ill family member. The result: only 14 percent of the US workforce has access to employer-sponsored paid family leave.[20]

---

20   Trish Stroman, Wendy Woods, Gabrielle Fitzgerald, Shalini Unnikrish-nan, and Liz Bird, "Why Paid Family Leave Is Good Business," Boston Consulting Group, February 7, 2017, www.bcg.com/publications/2017/ human-resources-people-organization-why-paid-family-leave-is-good-business.

There's greater pressure on working mothers in the US to self-support; many live far from their family of origin so are not able to call on other family members to help with childcare. American women face unique challenges and difficult decisions about whether to have children and what the trade-offs will be—financially, emotionally, and in terms of their career—if they do. As a result, American working mothers wrestle with guilt and worry about this decision-making in ways that women in other parts of the world do not.

Because I've lived and worked in other parts of the world, I recognize the cost of these public policies and what they communicate about the value of facilitating a more equal workplace. Americans who haven't had this more global perspective often don't understand how social systems in other countries offer very different forms of support for working parents, both men and women. In fact, it's more than the support; it's what these types of policies communicate about how the society views women. If a country does not offer paid parental leave, or childcare, or legislation mandating flex times, that country is communicating that a working mother is not an essential part of the economic system.

This is why it's important to think about cultural factors in any discussion of women and career growth. Consider your answers to these questions:

- Did you grow up in a country where family support and child-rearing were seen as collective responsibilities or a private issue?

- What do your country's public policies communicate about how women and child-rearing are viewed?

When you consider issues like affordable universal childcare, part-time and flexible work schedules, vacation and sick day provisions, and cash allowances to parents, it becomes clear that it's much easier to be a working mother in certain countries.

The COVID-19 pandemic has highlighted these inequities, and while the full impact will become clearer in the future, it is evident that childcare issues triggered by lockdowns and the shuttering of schools and day care facilities have played a significant role in women losing work, voluntarily and involuntarily. A Pew Research study found that American mothers of children twelve and under were three times more likely than fathers to have lost work between February and August 2020. Latina and Black women have borne a significant share of this job loss. In the US, women's labor force participation reached a thirty-three-year low in January 2021.[21] One in four women in the US are considering downshifting their careers or leaving the workforce entirely because of the impact of COVID-19.[22]

This is, of course, not simply an issue for American mothers. Globally, the pandemic has made it even harder for women to escape poverty.

I recognize the danger in writing about economic events in real time. And please understand: I don't want this chapter to become bogged down in political debates. My intent is to demonstrate that the ways in which you think about your career and mothering may be shaped as much by your country of origin or the country in which you are living and working as by your education, your peer group, or your employer's policies. As I shared at the beginning of this book, it's important to take a clear-eyed view of your culture and your working environment in order to shape effective strategies that will equip you for career growth.

---

21   Eliana Dockterman, "These Mothers Wanted to Care for Their Kids and Keep Their Jobs. Now They're Suing After Being Fired," *TIME*, March 3, 2021, https://time.com/5942117/mothers-fired-lawsuit-covid-19.

22   McKinsey & Company and Lean In, *Women in the Workplace 2020*.

I admire the work that Mary Catherine Bateson has done in this space. She was a writer and cultural anthropologist—and also the daughter of the well-known anthropologist Margaret Mead. She discussed the idea of cultural factors in this way:[23]

> I like to think of men and women as artists of their own lives, working with what comes to hand through accident or talent to compose and recompose a pattern in time that expresses who they are and what they believe in, making meaning even as they are studying and working and raising children, creating and recreating themselves.

What's profound about this quote is the sense of creativity and fluidity, the understanding that we are composing our lives in a very active way, using the tools we've been given and within the framework in which we find ourselves—the cultural context.

MY PERSPECTIVE

Let me refer to the question at the start of the chapter and share some personal perspective on this topic. For me, being a good mother meant that I would have a domestic life like that of my mother (one characterized by a position of White, middle-class privilege, which certainly is my story). I would have a beautiful home, host wonderful dinner parties, be highly engaged in my children's sporting and school lives, and be a rock for the extended family of aunts, uncles, and cousins. My mother was always home when I returned from elementary school; she was always available when her children needed her. She woke us up each morning by serving us a cup of tea in bed. She was my biggest cheerleader.

---

23   Mary Catherine Bateson, quoted in "On Being with Krista Tippett,"
      last updated December 21, 2020, https://onbeing.org/programs/
      mary-catherine-bateson-composing-a-life-aug2017.

So, this was a key part of my understanding of what my life should look like. But there was more. I also wanted to have a professional life like my father's. My father was a very well-respected anesthesiologist in South Africa. He was an expert who looked after his family and provided for them financially.

To me, being a good mother to my two sons meant that I should be able to do both of those things. I wanted them to have a mother who was deeply loving and always available—who woke them up with a cup of tea while they were still in bed—but at the same time, I also wanted them to have a mother who would be able to look after their financial needs, a mother whose career they could truly respect, as I did my father's.

I deeply appreciated how my mother showed up as a mother; her focus on us as her number one priority gave us all a strong confidence to face the world. She gave us a sense of invincibility and the knowledge that there was a place to retreat to if we needed to lick wounds or wanted some bolstering.

That's what I wanted for my sons—for them to know that they are fiercely loved, that I see them as remarkable people. I wanted that combination of love, attention, and interest in who they are to give them a grounded sense of self, the confidence to do the things they feel are important and meaningful, and to face anything that comes at them along their path. And, of course, to know that there is always a place to come home to, a place where they can find succor.

As for my father, a man who was respected both inside and outside our home, I admired the laser focus he was able to bring to his work. No one called him if they forgot their sports clothes. He came home at night with fascinating stories "of the world" that he shared at dinner, and as a curious kid, I learned so much through his experiences—the people he met, the things that challenged him. These experiences helped him identify patterns and form reasoned responses.

This is what shaped what I wanted for myself and for my relationships with my sons: to have the mind space to be reasonably focused on work, to have an impact in an area that people find of value, and for my sons to see me navigating "the world"—ideally, their world. To understand their challenges, their hopes, their aspirations, what the world looks like to them and how it operates, and then to hopefully add credible guidance and insights and to celebrate as they navigate it.

Perhaps you identify with my perspective. Perhaps you are striving to balance this idea of an impossible ideal ... plus more. It creates tremendous pressure, doesn't it, this belief that a good mother requires perfection *plus*.

Later in the book, I'll talk more about the transition from perfection to passion, but for now let's just acknowledge that you won't be able to move forward in your career if your attention is focused on this sense of never being enough, of searching for some magic formula or recipe or strategy that will make you better.

I've spoken earlier in this book about my grandmother and her importance as a role model for me. My mother was also a key role model. Her feelings about career and life were more complicated. While we were growing up, she did not work formally outside the home for long periods of time; instead, she cobbled together entrepreneurial ventures. Today, she is actively engaged in running a nonprofit foundation. It's become clear to me how her choices were shaped by cultural factors and expectations for women in that time. Despite the grace with which she oversaw her home and family life, she must have frequently been frustrated. She would have been a formidable businesswoman.

But her message to me was always clear: You are going to have a career. This message—you will have a career—was one cultural factor that shaped my choices and decision-making. Like many girls my age in South Africa, I also grew up with a second message, from my mother and others: You need to have your own bank account. I remember this quite clearly; it was considered vitally important for young women to have their own bank account, one that their partner did not know about.

These two factors were critical pieces of advice I was given by my mother: have a career and have your own bank account.

Yet other messages from my mother have shaped my decision-making around motherhood. When my sons were younger and were at home with a nanny while I worked late, she would phone me and ask why I wasn't at home instead of still in the office. There was a stage, if she was visiting, when she would tease me to put on some lipstick before my husband got home. She understands the value of work and the importance of a career, but like so many of us, she is still struggling to understand how to balance career, motherhood, and having a spouse or partner as well as how to identify the trade-offs that make sense.

My formative years were spent in a girls' boarding school. Our headmistress didn't allow any male teachers at the school. There was only one man on campus; he was the groundskeeper, and we weren't allowed near him. As a result, during these important years, I saw only women authority figures. It was women who taught science and math. It was women who coached our sports teams. We were disciplined with a ruler by the headmistress. At that school, women were in charge and held all the power—all around me, I had examples of powerful females.

We wore a strict uniform, with long skirts and knee socks. Even our underwear—hideously ugly bloomers—was mandated. Hairstyles were also regulated—you could wear your hair short, one ponytail, pigtails, or braids.

I share this not only because of the importance of female authority figures at this key time in my life but also because of the freedom that I found in this environment. I did not care what I looked like. My only concession to grooming was to shave my knees because that was the only part of my body that peeked out from the uniform. We all were dressed in nearly identical fashions. We all looked the same, and we all looked terrible.

The way you differentiated yourself was through your skills or talent. You were recognized and admired for the aspects that were uniquely you—your sense of humor or the musical instrument you played or the sport in which you participated or the class in which you excelled. I found that unbelievably liberating, and I know that it played a role in how I understood myself as a woman and what was possible.

Literature has also influenced me. I've been shaped by my reading about strong women, from Nancy Drew and *Little Women*'s Jo March to Lizzie Bennet from *Pride and Prejudice*. All of these books featured women as powerful, strong characters who, regardless of the environment they found themselves in, managed to speak out and do extraor-dinary things. Looking into the leadership ranks, when I started working, I missed the strong female role models that had shaped  my earlier life, but I found them in biographies—the accounts of women who had taken up their body of work with great intention and walked a path before me, lighting the way for those who wanted to take themselves up in a similar fashion. Through their biographies and memoirs, these women were like mentors and role models for me, teaching me not just how to live but how to express myself professionally, how to build a life and a career. Women like Mary Catherine Bateson, whose quote I used earlier, as well as Katharine

Graham, Lee Miller, Frida Kahlo, Georgia O'Keeffe, Swanee Hunt, Helen Thomas, Kathleen Norris, Pema Chödrön, and Joan Didion. Their stories showed me how women can live and take themselves up professionally.

In my work at the university, I like to ask my students which figures in their lives have made an impact on them. Many of them name people like Shonda Rhimes, Glennon Doyle, Issa Rae, Amy Cuddy, Brené Brown, Roxane Gay, Mel Robbins, Elizabeth Gilbert, Amanda Gorman, Stacey Abrams, and Naomi Osaka. Once they have their list, I encourage students to consider how their choices may have been shaped by these people who have influenced them. I also ask them to process the significance of who those people were when they were younger and what insights they can gain from how the people they read about have changed with the passage of time.

I want to invite you to pause and reflect on this yourself. Who were the characters whose stories you loved when you were young? Who are the women—real or fictional—whose stories are inspiring you today?

DIFFERENT CULTURES, DIFFERENT CHOICES

I met my husband, Chris, at our very first dance during our first year of college. We've been married now for more than twenty-five years; we've been together far longer than we've lived independently. We shared all of our firsts—first jobs, first credit cards, first promotions, first homes. We've lived on three continents and raised two sons and cared for multiple pets. We've ultimately shifted roles many times, changing who was the primary breadwinner and who stayed at home, who was a full-time employee and who was the contract worker, even whose career determined where we lived.

Like many of you, I was determined to have an egalitarian marriage when Chris and I first wed. I was relentless in my conviction that everything had to be fully fifty-fifty. If I poured Chris a cup of coffee, I insisted that he needed to pour me the next cup of coffee. If I made the bed, I made sure that he was the one who made the bed the next day.

It was a comment from a colleague that suggested that my focus on fifty-fifty was misplaced. They heard me enthusiastically discussing this approach to marriage and asked, "Do you only want half a marriage?" Instead of fifty-fifty, they said, why don't you go all in? Why don't you respond from a position of doing 100 percent of what's needed and trusting your partner to also provide 100 percent?

It was beautiful advice, and I wish that I could tell you that I was immediately convinced—that I altered my fifty-fifty approach and instead gave up keeping a tally of who served whom a cup of coffee and whose turn it was to make the bed.

But that would be dishonest. I admired the advice, knew that it was well meaning, and continued to ensure that our house operated on a fifty-fifty schedule.

I was married for about four years when I discovered that I was pregnant. I was overwhelmed by so many different emotions and fears. I made a determination to this unborn child that I would take care of it, envisioning—as I noted earlier—a combination of the time and focus my mother had given and the financial security provided by my father. But I was surprised by how important it became to me to learn my baby's sex. I had this clear sense that I couldn't speak to my unborn child without knowing if it was a son or daughter.

I do so much work around gender today that it's fascinating and a little alarming to reflect on how critical I felt it was to my ability to communicate effectively while my baby was in utero. I didn't care what the baby's sex was—I simply believed that I couldn't communicate effectively without this knowledge. Talk about socialized expectations! Once I knew that my baby was a boy, my thought was, "Okay. Now I know how to talk to you."

Having a child was the greatest leveling experience of my life—nothing went as I had planned or thought, and that sense of lack of control continues to this day. I had expected a natural childbirth, but my son ended up requiring a Cesarean delivery. This tiny baby looked nothing like I had expected.

It may be that other mothers have similar experiences and just don't talk about them, but when we discuss how cultural factors shape our careers, it's important to acknowledge the fact that sometimes we can't plan or control or shape a specific chapter. Sometimes people choose to show up and act in ways that are outside of your control. Sometimes those people are adults, and sometimes they are infants. The only solution is to take a deep breath and acknowledge that it is much easier to focus primarily on what you *can* control.

I've noticed that women tend to explain their employment opportunities through the lens of family. I am no exception. While pregnant, I made the decision to move from a corporate job with an insurance company to a university role because I thought it would be more family friendly. It's amazing to think of it now: The university employed me knowing I was pregnant. I was hired to work in an academic department staffed largely by older male professors; the head of the department was an elderly, conservative professor named Barend Lessing.

The clients I work with in America share that they are routinely told not to reveal to employers or prospective employers that they are pregnant. Just Google the topic "How to tell your boss that you are pregnant" and you'll see a fairly grim list of recommendations. There are still almost forty countries where women can be fired from their jobs simply for getting pregnant.[24]

This is why I say that cultural factors matter when it comes to career. It may have been in part the communal attitude in South Africa, but my boss not only hired me while pregnant but also he and my work colleagues could not have been more accommodating. He installed a large nursing chair in my office. My student assistant, a young man named Charles Kotze, would help transport my baby to and from the university and would mind him during the periods between classes. If the baby fell asleep, I'd put him at the base of the podium and carry on teaching and then take him home with me at the end of the day. My workplace was remarkably supportive in what was a very conservative country and a conservative time. In fact, having a child gave me an unexpected kind of "street cred" with my colleagues; they acted as if I had finally grown up.

I was fortunate to be able to afford a nanny, who helped care for the house and the baby—she was even the one who taught me how to nurse. We had affordable housing and parents nearby, and there was an older Lebanese woman who lived next door and would pop around with chicken soup.

I've mentioned before that South Africans are very communal. In my native country, there's a concept called "ubuntu," which represents the idea that we are all bound together. It's part of a Zulu phrase that can be translated as "I am because you are," or a person is a person through other people. This sense of shared humanity forms a stark contrast with the radical individualism I have found in the US.

When my son was eighteen months old, we moved to the UK, where I had my second son and discovered that the high cost of

---

24   Kathleen Hays and Michael Heath, "Women Can Be Fired for
      Pregnancy in 28 Nations, says World Bank's Reinhart," MoneyWeb,
      March 8 2021, www.moneyweb.co.za/news/companies-and-deals/
      women-can-be-fired-for-pregnancy-in-28-nations-says-world-banks-reinhart.

childcare meant that it was more cost-effective for me to stay at home and care for both boys, since I was earning less than my husband at the time. It was a rude awakening. Far from the support of extended family, I was for the first time fully responsible for my sons' care.

We lived in a commuter village outside London; my husband traveled into the city to work. I gradually formed a network of friendships with some of the other stay-at-home mothers who lived nearby. And what I discovered was a group of unbelievably competent women, all of whom were at home with the children because they were all in the same boat: it makes no sense to pay more for childcare than your salary. It gets dark early in London, especially in winter. By 4:00 p.m. the sun is setting, and we would gather in each other's homes and share our exhaustion over spending a day in the kind of domestic tasks we had never envisioned for ourselves. It was my first exposure to the "taking the edge off" culture or "wine mom" culture—overqualified women, spending time at home being quite depressed, who would sit drinking wine in chicken-nugget-strewn kitchens.

It was a noteworthy exposure to how cultural factors shape women's ability to pursue meaningful careers. I was still working remotely for the university, although only part-time and on a contract basis. But I had gone from having all of this support to performing the juggling act I see so many women doing, trying to balance childcare and work responsibilities. We'd gone from a very egalitarian marriage to a relatively traditional marriage in which my husband worked outside while I stayed at home and did the washing, cooking, and cleaning. And while this was my experience and that of my particular circle of friends, there were couples we knew who did make the choice to spend more on childcare than one partner earned so that they could both stay in the workforce and neither of them would have to struggle with career reentry.

But, as I shared earlier, my plan had been to have a domestic life like my mother and a work life like my father. And this, of course, meant impossibly high standards at home and at work. So, it's important for me to acknowledge that this opportunity to step back and take some of that pressure off was a relief in many ways. It is difficult to be fully immersed in both of those worlds.

At some deep level, I believed that my career aspirations were selfish. I had a sense that I could take all of my ambition and channel it into mothering, ignoring the complications inherent in that kind of intensive parenting.

During this season, and when I first arrived in the US, given visa requirements, I could not work full-time outside the home. These kinds of choices are not easy. They can change the power dynamics in a partnership. They can change your career trajectory.

Perhaps you can identify with the frustration that happens in these shifts and the guilt that often accompanies it.

I have many happy memories of time spent with my boys during this chapter of my life—of adventures and travel and trips to the park. But I did view it as a sacrifice on my part. I gave up where my career was going to be at home with them. And what I've recently learned is that my boys have no memory of it at all. They don't remember me being at home with them; their only memories are of me as a working mom.

FIGURE IT OUT

We moved to the United States as part of our goal to experience life in many different cultural environments. When we came here in 2001, our plan was to stay for a year and then move back to South Africa.

Twenty years later, this is our home.

Chris was viewed as more employable at the time, and he was the one to get a job here first. Because of visa requirements, my passport was stamped with a phrase that upsets me to this day: "Dependent Spouse." To be labeled as such felt like a sentence, that I was in some way giving up freedom and that my personhood could be defined only through and by my relationship to my spouse. That my value would be as Chris's appendage, not as a separate standing person who had something to bring to the world that could be considered of any import.

Gradually, I was able to change my work status. What has defined my working experience in the US is an interesting observation that women are expected to "figure it out" in a very individual way. Struggling, in isolation, with the same issue I was: work-life integration—how to have a family and a career that were both meaningful.

Many of the women I've coached who are in very senior positions have been clear that, at the time, the way to achieve what they did was by making the choice not to have children. More recently, we've seen a generation of women come through with children, but if you look more closely, many of them have stay-at-home partners or a significant amount of family support.

American women are largely doing this alone.

I said at the beginning of this book that part of my purpose is to equip you to take a clear, careful look at the environment in which you are operating, both personally and professionally. Cultural factors matter in this consideration.

In many other countries, the message behind public policies is that women are valued, their contribution is important, and they need to be part of the economy. Social programs are created to communally look after everyone so that women and working parents can actively participate in that economy.

In the United States, where there is a far greater value placed on individualism, there is an attitude that having children and participating in the economy are individual choices. As a result, each individual—each woman—must figure it out for herself. Companies may offer a brief leave; some may provide on-site care or flex time, but these are, again, decisions made on an individual level by individual companies. There is not a national conversation about creating an environment in which there is support—in terms of childcare and healthcare and leave and flexible working—for those individual choices.

The average age of students in the MBA program where I teach is twenty-seven. At twenty-seven, the women who attend our business school are committing to two years of study, graduating when they are twenty-nine or thirty. When they leave, they feel pressure to get a return on the money they've invested in their degree program. How can they fit in a family, if that is something that matters to them?

There are so many cultural assumptions around working women and around motherhood. The purpose of this discussion is not necessarily to advocate for one culture over another or for one specific set of public policies. Instead, I want to help you understand how to make sense of your life.

I encourage you to consider the ways in which your cultural identity has shaped how you think about what's possible. Our families, our stories, and our goals are all unique, and the choices we make are not necessarily static.

But it's vital to be purposeful in making those choices and to understand how your employer, and even the country where you live, can support you in making your goals possible. When you begin to understand

> **Our families, our stories, and our goals are all unique, and the choices we make are not necessarily static.**

your career choices within a cultural context, a public policy context, and where you are in your career cycle or life stage, you will be more forgiving of yourself and energized for the challenges ahead.

Reflection Points

1. How do your thoughts about motherhood and a meaningful career reflect your culture and how you were socialized?

_____

_____

_____

_____

_____

2. What do your country's public policies communicate about the value of facilitating a more equal workplace?

_____

_____

_____

_____

_____

3. Who are the women—real or fictional—whose stories have inspired you ?

CHAPTER THREE

YOUR TURN

Take a Good Look in the Mirror

*Our identity is both a reflection of what we do for a
living and a projection of how we wish to be perceived
and valued and recognized in the world.*

–ELIZABETH PERLE MCKENNA

When my eldest son was young, we had a favorite activity:
creating a self-portrait.

I viewed it as an "identity development" exercise, but
in reality, it was simply an activity we both loved. I would
lay my toddler down on a large piece of paper and trace his entire
body. He would then draw and color the details of
how he saw himself on this cutout—adding blue
eyes, blond hair, the cutest nose, maybe even his *Bob
the Builder* T-shirt.

You should try it. There is something really fun
and engaging about catching sight of yourself from
this angle. Yes, your waist may look a bit big, and

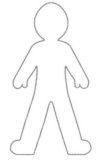

who knew that you had such a funny-shaped head? But there is your heart, and over there we can add a tattoo, if you would like.

It's tricky, but not impossible, to trace yourself in this way. You can find large rolls of tracing paper or construction paper. I encourage you to make the effort.

The most engaging part of this exercise is not in perfectly capturing your outline. Instead, it has to do with filling in the details, catching sight of your unique quirks and traits. The process of making yourself real. It is, in a sense, a process of transformation whereby the personal or private and seemingly unconscious comes into the light.

I find examples of the type of installation art that deals with undifferentiated cutout human forms equally compelling. I think here of the first time I caught sight of Ray Smith's *The Red Army*, which features more than nine hundred cutout steel figures gleaming red in a verdant field in Pennsylvania. Row after marching row of the same arms raised in silhouette. It is unclear whether their arms are raised in celebration or terror, and the result is both unsettling and oddly beautiful.

Or there is the soft roundness of the haunting forms of Antony Gormley's *Another Place*. This modern sculpture features sea swirling and barnacles settling on each of the one hundred cast-iron figures spread out along three kilometers of beach—all looking out to sea. Some of the figures are submerged, depending on the ebb and flow of tides. There is something poignant about these stark figures, all staring at the horizon.

I've frequently walked along the Allegheny River to admire *Unkillable Human* by Frederick Franck: a solid rectangular steel plate with its interior cut out in the outline of a human form surrounded by flames of steel. The image apparently burned in the artist's memory after visiting Hiroshima. Walking farther along the path, you find the standing, retrieved, inner steel cutout of the human image rising like a phoenix from the ashes. It's a heart-wrenching piece of art.

These images, on the one hand, are compelling because I recognize the human form, the fallibility and comfort of that, but at the same time, there is a bleakness, an emptiness, a hollowness, as the details are not here. Who were and are they? What's their story? Where are the scars and the bumps and the laughter?

In this chapter, I want to encourage you to fill in those

details. To take a good look at who you are—the messiness, the roots, the weeds, the beauty. We are going to give life and color and clarity to your cutout form by looking at the things you do.

You come to understand yourself by looking at your life: your relationships, your activities, and your interests. It's not a matter of introspection or looking inside yourself, finding some deeply hidden treasure, but of circumspection and recognition—looking out into your world, paying attention to your life involvements, and then seeing yourself in and through what you do.

So often, in executive coaching situations, when you ask someone who they are, they'll tell you who they would like to be. The list sounds awfully familiar in a Girl Guide/Boy Scout kind of way: I'm trustworthy, loyal, helpful, courteous, kind, obedient, cheerful, thrifty, brave, clean, reverent, etc. In contrast, some clients will tell you who others think they are. Neither is particularly helpful if change, development, and growth are your goals.

As management consultant Meg Wheatley explains:[25]

> *I can only change how I act if I stay aware of my beliefs and assumptions. Thoughts always reveal themselves in behavior. As humans we often contradict ourselves—we say one thing and do another—we state who we are but then act contrary to that. We say we are open-minded but then judge someone for their appearance. We say we are a team but then gossip about a colleague. If we want to change our behavior, we need to notice our actions and see if we can uncover the belief that led to that response. What caused me to behave that way and not some other way.*

---

25   Margaret J. Wheatley, *Turning to One Another: Simple Conversations to Restore Hope to the Future* (San Francisco: Berrett-Koehler, 2002).

I believe that if you want to know who you are, look at what you do. That's more telling than anything else. It's also true that if you begin your focus with the nitty-gritty actions of your life, you can then create and articulate a future vision that is grounded, not some airy-fairy version of who you would like to be that is unrelated to the reality of your world. By working through a type of "practice inspection" process, you will also gain clarity not only on what you want but also on why you want it and what purpose you will fulfill in having it.

Think of this process of inspecting the things you do as a closet spring cleaning. I know, I know … nobody ever really feels like doing that. It takes motivation to open that closet and start with the top shelf. Or perhaps you start with your shoes. There is dust in the corners back there. And then there are the decisions. Will you ever really wear that again? Is it okay to be nostalgic and keep that leather bomber jacket, or should you toss it? Somewhere in the middle, you lose momentum, and it seems all uphill, and you need to drink copious amounts of tea and break for at least one hefty sandwich.

But think about what follows when you are finished: a wonderful, light feeling. Space, order, and alignment. Everything in its place. Folded and sorted. And the best of intentions to keep it this way forever.

Here, in this chapter, it's all about you. This also requires a systematic process. A process of self-observation, honest description, and thoughtful reflection. It takes time, but it can dramatically and positively affect every aspect of your life.

Be assured that although the process is thorough, it certainly is not tedious. Making carefully considered choices about how you define yourself is fundamentally creative and allows you to connect with your life again.

Who you are implies who you have been and who you may become. What you do now makes sense because of your past experience and has significance in relation to what you anticipate doing in the future.

> **Who you are implies who you have been and who you may become.**

In reflecting on what you do, you reflect on your beliefs, you give thought to the decisions you have made, and you identify current options. You make choices for the future. These will become the driving force—your commitment to a different future.

COMPOSING A SELF-PORTRAIT

We have spent a lot of time in this book discussing what could be the unconscious biases at play in your environment—the factors that may impede you from getting to where you want to be. But there is a second critical element that I want to discuss now: you will need to look at the parts of you that aren't growing in the direction you need them to grow.

What does this mean? I'm talking here about the concept of "getting stuck," and it's a concept that's not unique to women. All genders get stuck. This is the reality that what got you *here* won't get you *there*. You may have become an expert in your current role and still be unable to move forward.

This is particularly true if you're looking at leadership roles. The skill sets that have equipped you to be successful are not necessarily the skill sets that let you move to the next level. You need different skill sets.

You may feel that you want to or should be at a different level or in a different position. You may be a highly effective individual contributor. But more is needed for a leadership role.

That's why I'm encouraging you to consider your professional identity as you compose your self-portrait. It's vital to reflect on who you are but then to acknowledge that you need to outgrow who you are in order to move on to a different level.

Let's spend a few minutes reflecting on some questions that may help you understand whether you've outgrown your professional identity and whether it's time to take your skill sets to a different place or develop new ones. Consider carefully your answers:

- Have you had to downsize your ambition? How so?

- Are you losing sight of your aspirations? Why do you think that is?

- Are you losing faith in your dreams? Why do you think that is?

- Do you feel stalled or sidelined? How so?

- Would you describe yourself as ambitious but going nowhere? Or are there other adjectives you would use? Why would you describe yourself this way?

- Do you see signs that your career prospects are constrained? If so, what are they?

- Have you been passed over or closed out of top jobs? If so, why do you think that is?

It can be challenging—even painful—to do this kind of thoughtful reflection. But in parallel, or as a separate exercise, please consider your answers to these questions as well:

- Who do you want to be—what are your goals, aspirations, and dreams?

- Who can you be—what are your potentials, capacities, skills, obstacles, and fears?

- Are you living the life that you want? Are you successful in what you do? Are you filling the roles and involved in the relationships that fulfill you?

I find William Bridges's work on managing change and transitions helpful as I coach clients. I've adapted these questions from his work, and you may find them helpful to consider as you navigate a career transition.[26]

Begin by considering this: If you're not where you want to be, why? If you want to transition to the next leadership level, what should you be focusing on?

1. Do you think you may be bumping up against gender stereotypes and the double bind? Remember the questions we discussed earlier in the book and consider your responses, contrasting your response today with how you would have responded when you started your career:

    □ Do you aspire to top management within the company?

    □ Do you have the confidence you can reach top management?

2. Have you perhaps outgrown your professional identity?

    □ What's the signal that the time has come to stop inhabiting your current role in a specific way?

    □ What's not working?

3. What has to happen so that you can take the next step in your story?

---

26 William Bridges, *Managing Transitions: Making the Most of Change* (Cambridge, MA: Da Capo Press, 2003).

4. What is it time to let go of? (This should be something internal, not an external step like leaving a job.)

   ▫ Something you have believed or assumed?

   ▫ Some way you have always been or seen yourself?

   ▫ Some outlook on the world?

   ▫ An attitude toward others/an assumption about others?

   ▫ A style of responding to challenges?

   ▫ A goal or dream for the future?

Once you have your answers to these questions, reflect on them. What are three things you have learned about yourself? Two things that you are excited about sharing with others? Did completing this exercise make you ask any other questions of yourself, or are there any questions you still have? What are they, and how would you answer them?

COLLECTING FEEDBACK

Women don't get enough feedback.

It doesn't matter what you intend or how you think you're showing up as a person or as a worker or a leader. If it's not being perceived that way in your workplace, that's a problem.

As you consider your self-portrait, it's helpful to reflect on whether you're stuck and determine whether you've outgrown where you are. But the next step is to check in on your environment and get feedback from that environment.

There's something valuable in understanding precisely how you are viewed. This understanding will be critical to your ability to identify why you may be stuck and what skills you need to build to move forward. Even if the feedback you receive is very positive, it will help you understand how others perceive you.

It's important to take time for this—to consider why you may not be where you want to be. There are likely some gender-related issues that stand in your way, but there may be an element of who you are that has not grown in some time. It's also possible that you've grown, but you haven't communicated that to anyone. Now is the time to get feedback from other people to identify what you should be doing in order to move forward.

I encourage you to gather feedback outside of a normal performance management process. It may be helpful to ask for feedback if you're working on a specific project or if you're considering moving into a new role. You'll want to know what the perceptions are of you and the challenges you may face in moving into this new opportunity.

I understand. We get nervous asking for feedback. We never want to hear bad things, so we don't ask. But then, when you fail to ask, you are not told.

One of the legacies of the #MeToo movement is that men are reluctant to engage with women, especially in one-on-one meetings with no others present, and so there are fewer opportunities for men to give women feedback. American male managers also have revealed that they are afraid of how women will respond to negative feedback and critical performance assessments. Coupled with the reactions to the #MeToo movement, along with the differences in how feedback has traditionally been given, men give other men feedback more easily, and it tends to center around specific skills—things they could be doing to improve their development.[27]

In contrast, the feedback women receive often centers around

---

27   Tim Bower, "The #MeToo Backlash," *Harvard Business Review,* September-October 2019, https://hbr.org/2019/09/the-metoo-backlash.

style and is anchored in gender stereotypes—women are described as too nice, or too aggressive, or too bossy. What do you do with that kind of feedback? It's a clear difference—men get feedback more often, they get feedback more directly, and they get feedback that helps their career.

The solution is for you to ask for feedback that is specific and that can inform how you prepare for new roles and new opportunities. One strategy is to request feedback in the form of three positives and three negatives. Ask for three examples of things you did well and three areas that offer "opportunities for improvement."

When you do this, you are giving them permission to give you that feedback. You are inviting them to share their observations. The number three is arbitrary, but it creates some context for the person providing the feedback—it invites more than simply a surface-level comment.

How you respond to feedback is also important. Negative feedback can be unexpected, even hurtful.

It's difficult to receive feedback well. I urge my students and clients to simply say, "Thank you."

"Thank you" is a neutral, deescalating phrase. It doesn't imply acceptance or agreement. You are simply acknowledging that feedback has been given.

You may choose to say, "Thank you; I hadn't thought about it that way." Again, this response doesn't mean "I agree." It also doesn't imply "I'm going to work on that immediately." It's simply a graceful response to the feedback that has been provided.

If you do not have a formal way of gathering this kind of feedback in your organization, I encourage you to write an email asking eight to ten people whose opinions and insights you trust for feedback on the passions, qualities, traits, and abilities that they appreciate in you or find of value. These people should be a mix of personal and professional contacts; your goal is to find patterns in the feedback through the descriptions and phrases that are used.

Your request for feedback might look a bit like this:

Dear _____,

I'm wondering if I might ask you for some help? I have been reflecting on my [professional development/leadership brand/fill in the blank] and would appreciate it if you would share a story, insights, or examples of when you think I was/am at my best.

I'd be very interested in what you see as my talents, my abilities, my passions. Are there characteristics that best describe me? What am I good at? How do I do things? What can you count on me for? Are there distinguishing characteristics that you see about who I am that you'd be willing to share?

Thanks for your support.

One client I worked with—I'll call her Cassie—invited feedback like this from family, friends, work colleagues, and her boss. Here are some samples of the feedback she received:

I met Cassie when her family moved from Ohio in the early 1980s. I have seen her grow as a woman, and I am proud to call her my friend. In high school, she overcame a life-threatening obstacle. I watched as she went through each day with an attitude of "I will not quit." I really admired her tenacity during that time and through to the present day.

One of Cassie's talents is the ability to really listen to people. I have been to many social gatherings with Cassie over the years, and she has many friends because of her ability to listen.

Family is very important to Cassie, and that is her passion. She is very reliable and is always willing to lend a helping hand. Another passion that Cassie has is to be healthy and exercise.

Cassie adopted two children, which was an enormous undertaking. This shows that she is extremely organized and sees things through to their completion. Cassie is also a good leader and works hard at every job or project that she takes on.

I most admire Cassie's ability to remain positive and upbeat in stressful times. I know that she is not immune to stress and feels it every bit as much as we all do, but she can quickly determine what needs to be done and calmly develops an action plan. She doesn't take the issues/concerns personally, which is often hard not to do. She realizes that it's about the job, not about her. That helps to set the tone for the rest of the group.

Cassie is passionate about her job but even more so she is passionate about her family. She manages the work/life balance issues in an extremely motivating way—she is up front about her family commitment but in a way that you never question her work commitment. She manages to do a terrific job at both! She is a role model for others (especially women) at our company.

And from her boss:

First let me say this: Cassie is a good person. How would I define a good person? First, a good mom and a good wife. Second, Cassie maintains strong family ties with her parents and siblings. Cassie is also honest and extremely ethical in her personal as well as business relationships. Cassie's peers respect her and her abilities. Cassie is a go-to person for advice and knowledge.

Cassie has an ability to actually receive constructive advice and make the suggested changes. Cassie has fun at what she does— she doesn't take herself too seriously—she can laugh at her own mistakes. But she takes her responsibilities very seriously. She lives up to her commitments and delivers on her key business goals. Cassie does not shy away from issues that need resolving. Her staff like working for her.

Despite the fact that her feedback providers knew her in very different contexts, there was a consistent reflection of the same traits, abilities, and passions. She was described as a woman who was brave, driven, and organized. A good manager. A compassionate, fun-loving, diligent individual who was confident and comfortable in the give-and-take world that characterized her workplace. A woman who placed strong emphasis on family.

They were all very positive traits, but for Cassie, this picture presented a problem. She wanted to advance in her career to an executive level, but what she understood from the feedback was that while she was perceived as solid and reliable, she was not seen as the innovative and visionary thinker that she knew her organization valued in their senior leaders. She needed to position herself differently in the marketplace in order to be seen as possessing executive-level skills and traits.

This is why I'm encouraging you to gather feedback. Request it from family, friends, colleagues, and supervisors.

After you have received your feedback, examine it carefully, looking for uniformity of phrases or concepts. Are there any red flags? What picture emerges of you, and how does it compare with the self-portrait you composed earlier? Does this picture best represent who you are and what you can do? Does it create value in the eyes of the organization you work for and its key stakeholders? Does this picture reveal any risks you're taking on? Does it align with the future you hope to create for yourself? If not, what are your goals for future development?

If you are considering taking on a new role, make a list of the skills and traits that an ideal candidate for that position should have. Then compare this target list with the feedback you've received. A reality test, if you will.

There's tremendous worth in understanding the perceived value you bring, in asking how people see you and beginning to identify what you should do more of and where you need to begin making a shift. The gathering of feedback is vital because we do not get enough of it, but it's also important in a context of intention versus perception.

HOW I SEE ME	HOW YOU SEE ME
Shy	Aloof
Upbeat	Phony
Spontaneous	Flakey
Truth teller	Nasty
Passionate	Emotional
Smart	Arrogant
High standards	Hypercritical
Outgoing	Overbearing

Take a look at this table; notice the differences between the words in the left column and the words in the right. We judge ourselves on our intentions while others tend to judge us on our behaviors/impact.[28] What you intend doesn't mean anything if it's not how you are being perceived.

What you intend doesn't mean anything if it's not how you are being perceived.

---

28   Douglas Stone and Sheila Heen, *Thanks for the Feedback: The Science and Art of Receiving Feedback Well* (New York: Viking, 2014).

Reflection Points

1. What are the goals, aspirations, and dreams that matter most to you?

   _____

   _____

   _____

   _____

   _____

2. Which potentials, capacities, skills, obstacles, and fears are revealed in your self-portrait?

   _____

   _____

   _____

   _____

   _____

3. What traits and abilities are highlighted in the feedback you receive?

_____

_____

_____

_____

_____

4. Which skills do you need to build to transition to the next leadership level ?

_____

_____

_____

_____

_____

CHAPTER FOUR

YOU OWN YOUR CAREER

Success is a moving goal post. You celebrate in those moments and then look at what's next ... and how can I do it better than I did before.

—ISSA RAE

L et's begin this chapter with a stark truth: you need to take ownership of your career.

Many women believe that their career is in the hands of their current employer or supervisor. They think that their bosses spend time considering what's best for their employees—what they want in terms of their career and what they don't.

I admit that I am guilty of this, too. I assume that the person I report to is looking out for new opportunities for me, thinking about my career development, and each time an opening becomes available, carefully assessing whether or not I am the right match.

The reality is that, for most women, this is simply not true. Too often, supervisors only take time to reflect on our performance during a review cycle. Workplaces are busy, and generating new opportunities for employees seldom rises to a priority status when there are so many other problems to be solved.

That's why I've encouraged you to take the time to request and assess feedback in the last chapter. As you review feedback—particularly from a supervisor—you will see precisely how you are perceived in your workplace. Without feedback, too often you'll assume that your supervisor and colleagues see you as you see yourself. It can be shocking to read through their feedback and discover that their perceptions may not be as rosy as you thought.

You may discover that you're not valued in the way that you envisioned; it may not be your strategic thinking that is recognized in your workplace but your ability to reliably meet deadlines or complete projects or tasks that are less leadership oriented and more likely to result in a supervisor being quite happy to keep you in the role you are currently filling.

> You can and must take charge of your career rather than waiting to be recognized and rewarded.

You may discover that you're not on track to rise within the company as you had thought.

This can be a sobering discovery, but my message here is intended to be a wake-up call. You can and must take charge of your career rather than waiting to be recognized and rewarded.

LOCUS OF CONTROL

One of the reasons why women often fail to take charge of their careers is the principle of "locus of control." Locus of control is a psychological concept that explains whether we think we are in control of our lives or whether we are controlled by external factors. A locus of control scale is a form of measuring the extent to which individuals believe that their behavior influences their circumstances. If you have a stronger internal locus of control, you're more likely to believe that you "make life happen," whereas if you have a stronger external locus of control, you feel that "life happens to you."

It's clear why this matters when it comes to career opportunities and to the idea of owning your career. With an external locus of control, you will believe that you are at the whim of your environment, lacking the ability to take charge of your destiny. Your understanding is that the key to success and fulfillment in life is in the hands of someone else, maybe a supervisor, or the CEO, or a spouse or partner. You become a passive agent, waiting for your environment to change for the better.

People with an internal locus of control spontaneously undertake activities to advance their own interests more than people with an external locus of control. They are also more likely to seek out information in their environment that will help advance their goals, and they are more likely to be assertive to others. They may also be less vulnerable to negative feedback.

Sadly, women tend toward an external locus of control, believing that their circumstances are controlled by others, while men are more likely to believe that they can influence their circumstances and opportunities through their own actions. This is not just true of American women; the research was replicated in fourteen countries and controlled for occupational status. Female senior managers and unskilled workers saw themselves as having less control over their lives than men. I note here that even women in positions of power who exercise a great deal of control over their work role still believe that external forces influence their lives more than men in the same roles.[29]

29 Peter B. Smith, Shaun Dugan, and Fons Trompenaars, "Locus of Control and Affectivity by Gender and Occupational Status: A 14 Nation Study," *Sex Roles* 36 (1997): 51–77, https://doi.org/10.1007/BF02766238.

One of the most damning studies comes from the work of my colleague Linda Babcock at Carnegie Mellon's Leadership Academy.[30] When men and women are asked the question "Who decides what you are worth?" it's clear that men are operating from a position of far greater agency.

"I determine my own worth, and it is up to me to make sure that my company pays me what I'm worth." Eighty-five percent of men agreed with that statement. Only 17 percent of women agreed.

"My worth is determined by what my company pays me." Eighty-three percent of women agreed, compared with only 15 percent of men.

If we reflect on the fact that people with an internal locus of control spontaneously undertake efforts to advance their own interests more than people with an external locus of control—they're more likely to seek out information in their environment that will help advance their goals, are more likely to be assertive, and are less vulnerable to negative feedback—we can begin to recognize the importance of owning your career and why it's vital for women to begin to think differently. If the guy sitting at the desk next to you is looking for ways to advance his goals, acting assertively, and accepting and learning from negative feedback, and you aren't, his career will move forward in a very different way. These are behaviors that are vital for career success.

I think about my dad whenever I have these kinds of discussions. It may sound funny, but I can clearly identify the day that the locus of control light bulb switched on for me. I was in college, and I was complaining to my dad about something. He sat me down and told

---

30   Linda C. Babcock, Michele Joy Gelfand, Deborah Small, and Heidi Stayn, "Propensity to Initiate Negotiations: A New Look at Gender Variation in Negotiation Behavior" (Presentation, IACM 15th Annual Conference, Salt Lake City, UT, April 15, 2002).

me that I would never do what I needed to do in my life because I kept seeing situations as external to me. I viewed it as always someone else's fault, no matter the circumstances in which I found myself. He told me that, until I took responsibility for this, I would not be an adult. I would never have the life that I wanted. I would not be successful.

The day that my dad said this to me, it changed my life. I knew that I had to grow up, to take responsibility for where I was and who I wanted to be.

Please understand that I'm not simply saying to you, "Snap out of it! Change your locus of control and all will be well." It's hard work when your environment doesn't change with you but instead keeps attempting to put you into a position where you have little or no control. Ultimately it's the systems that need to change, but until they do, it's important to understand the impacts of engaging in certain behaviors.

MESSAGE IN THE MARBLE

In a way, it isn't surprising that so many women sense that their environments are hindering their ability to advance and achieve their goals. For generations, women have been held back, restricted, and required to battle to achieve their right to own property, to vote, to get access to birth control, to attend college, to earn a Bachelor of Science degree.

On the campus of Carnegie Mellon University is a beautiful building—the Margaret Morrison building. Margaret Morrison was the mother of Andrew Carnegie, one of the university's founders, and he dedicated the building to her as a way to honor his mother. At a time before women had the right to vote, they could attend the Margaret Morrison Carnegie School for Women and earn a three-year diploma or a two-year certificate. But these early pioneers had a limited curriculum: originally, the school offered only vocational courses that trained women to be librarians, secretaries, seamstresses, and bookkeepers.

Carved into the marble at the top of the dome on the Margaret Morrison building are these words: "These are woman's high prerogatives — To make and inspire the home — To lessen suffering and increase happiness — To aid mankind in its upward struggles — To ennoble and adorn life's work, however humble."

It's wild to see these words—these aspirations for women—carved into a building at one of the top technical universities in the country. But it's also a reminder that we stand on the shoulders of the women who came before us. They were pioneers. They needed to take charge of their lives and their careers in a time when a woman's greatest privileges were believed to center around homemaking and increasing the happiness of others.

Within the building itself, an alumna—Rebecca Deutsch—has created an extraordinary art display in the staircase. This installation depicts the voices of women students from the university and reflects the range of their experiences in a series of quotes. One from 1938 quotes a female student who applied to the dean to take advanced math and science courses and was told unequivocally no. Another is from a woman who had completed the requirements for a metallurgical degree but was instead awarded a degree in chemistry, since women weren't allowed to earn metallurgical degrees. Some quotes are positive, reflecting an experience of collaboration in the engineering department that transcended gender. The quotes are inserted into corners and odd angles, representing the experience of women who often feel sidelined in traditionally male-dominated industries and careers.

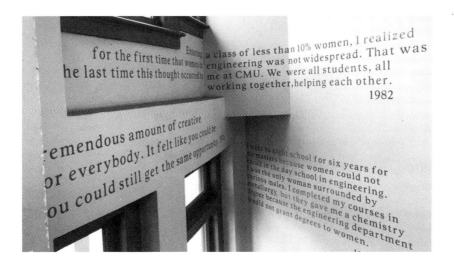

for the first time that women in engineering was not widespread. That was the last time this thought occurred to me at CMU. We were all students, all working together, helping each other.

1982

remendous amount of creative or everybody. It felt like you could be ou could still get the same opportunity.

I went to night school for six years for my masters because women could not enroll in the day school in engineering. I was the only woman surrounded by curious males. I completed my courses in metallurgy, but they gave me a chemistry degree because the engineering department would not grant degrees to women.

What's intriguing to me about this very visual representation is the fact that you look up and see this old-fashioned understanding of what women could be and then inside are the possibilities. Students look up, all around them, and see the evidence of the women who have gone before, the reminder that these women opened doors so that they would have even greater opportunities.

PARTNERING WELL

I want to pause here and talk for a moment about exercising agency in another area—your choice of whether or not to partner and who to partner with. Part of taking ownership of your choices in life involves building an understanding of how your relationships can impact your ability to advance in the workplace. I believe very strongly that should you choose to partner, who you partner with and how that plays out have an enormous impact on the success of your career. Facebook's COO, Sheryl Sandberg, makes a similar point when she says, "I truly believe that the single most important career decision that a woman makes is whether she will have a life partner and who that partner is."[31]

I think that this statement is true, regardless of your gender or the gender of your partner. Your choice of partner and who that person is will significantly impact your ability to be successful in your career and experience growth and fulfillment from new career opportunities. I see this in conversations with my sons. As they discuss their future plans—their aspirations for where they want to live and how they want to live and what they want to do—I've realized that these exciting aspirations no longer depend on parental support or encouragement. Who they partner with will significantly impact whether or not these dreams become reality.

I encourage you to confront this as part of your efforts to take ownership of your life and career. At the Tepper School, I teach workshops designed to equip more effective partnerships, enabling couples to have important conversations throughout the lifetime of their partnership on negotiating and finding common ground in three areas: values, boundaries, and fears.

My teaching here has been drawn from the work of Jennifer Petriglieri.[32] She's done amazing work in this space, identifying three key areas—values, boundaries, and fears. For a dual-career couple to work—in fact, for any couple to work—Petriglieri explains that they need to have conversations regularly around values, boundaries, and fears. I think it's interesting to consider each of these areas as a circle. The goals of those conversations should be to identify

---

31   Sheryl Sandberg, cited in Kathleen Elkins, "Warren Buffett and Sheryl Sandberg Agree on the Most Important Decision You Will Ever Make," CNBC, February 7, 2017, www.cnbc.com/2017/02/07/warren-buffett-and-sheryl-sandberg-agree-on-most-important-decision.html.

32   Jennifer Petriglieri, *Couples That Work: How Dual-Career Couples Can Thrive in Love and Work* (Boston: Harvard Business Review Press, 2019).

common ground—the areas where the circles overlap—because that alignment or overlap will make for a successful partnership and a successful work life.

What does this mean exactly? Values define the direction of your path, boundaries set its borders, and fears reveal the potential cliffs to avoid on either side. Sharing a clear view in these three domains will make it easier to negotiate and overcome the challenges you encounter together.

Let's take a moment and consider an exercise I do with my students, adapted from the work of Donald Sull and Dominic Houlder.[33]

Taking Stock Exercise

When you step back and take stock of your day-to-day actions, you may notice a gap between the things you value most and the way you actually spend your time, money, and attention. The gap raises questions about how you manage the differences between your professed values and your actual behavior.

---

33 Donald Sull and Dominic Houlder, "Do Your Commitments Match Your Convictions?" *Harvard Business Review*, January 2005, https://hbr.org/2005/01/do-your-commitments-match-your-convictions.

WHAT MATTERS MOST TO US (WHAT WE VALUE)	MONEY	TIME
Career growth/ professional development	2%–5% professional networks/ membership groups	5–8 hours/ month
Travel	5%	A trip each quarter
Financial planning and retirement	15% retirement savings	Monthly/ quarterly reviews
Exercise	1%–2%	5–10 hours/ week
Time with family and friends	Calls/meals	5–10 hours/ week
Kids' education	20%–25% college fees	
Spiritual development	2% retreats, learning materials, gifting	5–10 hours/ week

As part of the process of taking stock, it's important to consider what matters to you. Take a look at the sample chart I've provided and use it as a template for creating your own. I've found this exercise quite useful for couples, but in truth it holds a lot of value for any person regardless of their relationship status. When you think about what matters to you, you may want to prioritize career growth. You may place financial security on your chart or time with children. You may want time with your partner on your chart. Your chart might include an entry about launching a business or opportunities to travel.

Next, map out how much money and time you are spending on the areas you have listed as being most important to you.

Once you've completed your chart, consider whether or not you are living according to your values, either as an individual or as a couple. It's easy to talk about the things you value, but are you living in a way that reflects this importance? Are you dedicating the majority of your money, time, and energy to the things you say matter most?

It's important to spend time reflecting on these areas, because they do impact your ability to move forward effectively. Values are the yardsticks we use to measure our lives. When our choices and actions align with our values, we feel content. When they don't, we feel stressed and unhappy.

> **Values are the yardsticks we use to measure our lives.**

My husband, Chris, and I could not be more different people; we came from different socioeconomic backgrounds, grew up speaking different home languages, and have different career, hobby, and sporting interests. However, we could not be more aligned on how we see education, family, ambition, ways to bring up children, and our belief in honoring the gifts you are given.

Harking back to Jennifer Petriglieri's work, values form one clear element, but boundaries and fears must also contain common ground. Setting clear boundaries together allows you to make big decisions more easily.

Consider three types of boundaries: place, time, and presence. One of the values Chris and I shared was a desire to travel, to live and work in different cultural environments. Another value was a solid educational experience for our sons. This meant that we occasionally took jobs that paid a bit less or that required one of us to be away from home for long stretches of time. We also identified the value of time with each other and time with our children, so we made the decision to work longer hours during weekdays in order to reserve the weekends for family time.

The final element here is fears. A strong partnership comes when you are able to ask each other, "What are your concerns for the future? What's your biggest fear about how our relationship and careers interact? What do you dread might happen in our lives?"

As you grow and experience career change, it's vital to have that check-in and the opportunity to examine how fears may impact your ability to move forward confidently. How will new responsibilities or a new role or a new job impact not just you but your partner?

These kinds of questions are also helpful to consider before you commit to a partnership. What impact will long hours or frequent travel or weekend responsibilities have on your ability to dedicate time or energy to a partner?

I feel that it's important here for me to acknowledge that I had the privilege of a supportive partner. I recognize that not every woman has the financial or emotional support from which I benefited as a wife and mother. But I share my story here to help illustrate the choices that I made and that we made as a couple and to reflect the knowledge that I took from those choices. It's all part of the process of taking ownership of where I am and who I am now and using that understanding to better move forward.

We now know that support and kindness are the two factors that most accurately predict the success of a working couple.[34] But our

---

34 Petriglieri, *Couples That Work.*

marriage's success is also attributed to what I call a certain amount of "delusion"—he thinks far more highly of me than I do of myself, and I admire him in the same way. I've seen fascinating research detailing what it takes to have a happy marriage.[35] The one consistency that emerged is that the partners in the marriage rated each other more positively than they rated themselves on every single quality being assessed. The researchers concluded that happily married couples write a generous narrative about each other—their stories focus on the most charitable explanation for each other's behavior, and they believe it. My husband's solid support—his belief that I am more capable than I have ever felt about myself—has been a career superpower for me.

TAKING CONTROL

I recognize that it can be challenging to take the kind of clear-eyed assessment of the choices you've made that have led you to where you are today. Reflecting on how gendered environments, cultural factors, and even your choice of partner have helped or hindered you is sobering. Reviewing feedback can be dispiriting, and it's depressing to recognize that other people don't care about your career in the same way that you do.

My message is not to plant yourself in an attitude of "nobody cares about me."

Instead, I want you to recognize that there are specific strategies you can begin to implement to build agency—to develop the mindset and the muscles that will shift your perspective. There are very corporate-facing techniques you can do that will help you begin

---

35 Sandra L. Murray, Dale W. Griffin, Jaye L. Derrick, Brianna Harris, Maya Aloni, and Sadie Leder, "Tempting Fate or Inviting Happiness? Unrealistic Idealization Prevents the Decline of Marital Satisfaction," *Psychological Science* 22, no. 5 (2011), https://doi.org/10.1177/0956797611403155.

CLIMBING THE SPIRAL STAIRCASE

to advocate for yourself. In the chapters ahead, we'll focus on the transitions you can make and the skills you can develop to accelerate your career in ways that are positive and exciting.

As you prepare to begin this transition, spend a few minutes reflecting on your answers to these questions:

- Do you usually wait to see what kind of raise you get, or do you try to negotiate in advance for the raise you think you deserve?

- Do you wait to be promoted or to be assigned more responsibilities, or do you ask for those things when you think you're ready?

- Do you think you're qualified to move up to the next level at work but assume your boss doesn't agree because they haven't promoted you yet?

- Have you accepted being given the same sort of work to do over and over again, even though you'd like to learn new skills and try different types of assignments?

- Do you typically ask for changes at work that would make your life more convenient, or do you tolerate small inconveniences even when you can see a simple fix?

- Have you identified the next step you want to take in your career? Does your supervisor know what you want to do?

- Do most of your colleagues perceive you as someone who's interested in moving ahead and performing at the next level of leadership, or are most of your coworkers unaware of your ambitions?

Your answers to these questions will help you begin to understand where you fall on the locus of control scale and will identify the skills you'll want to build to move forward. It's all about a stance of agency—how you stand in a career.

My goal for you is to stand in a way that equips you to advocate for yourself.

Consider carefully how you've answered the bulleted questions. We'll discuss negotiation later in this book; for now, let me simply say that changing your stance begins by *asking*.

Ask for the projects and assignments that match your skills and interests. Ask for more responsibility. Ask to be promoted before a promotion is offered.

Don't cede the responsibility for your career to someone else. Own your career, and advocate for yourself.

Reflection Points

1. What skills do you need to build to equip you to ask for more responsibilities and for projects that match your interests?

_____

_____

_____

_____

_____

2. Have you ceded responsibility for your career's growth and development to someone else?

_____

_____

_____

_____

_____

3. What specific "ask" are you inspired to try ?

_____

_____

_____

_____

_____

PART TWO
THE TRANSITIONS

D epending on where you find yourself in your career, you may need to make a transition to move to the next level. The three transitions I've identified in the chapters in this section each speak to a specific shift you must make to advance your career and to move away from strong individual contributor levels of competence and into ways of thinking about yourself and acting as a leader.

In the next three chapters, I'll discuss these transitions in greater depth, but I encourage you to pause here and consider which transition you need to make. The transition that's required may reflect where you are in your career. Are you at an early stage in your working life and discovering that you need to move from a focus on being perfect at your job to being passionate about your career? Are you spending too much time working on tasks and projects and not enough time building networks of influence? Are you viewed in your workplace as an effective implementor of programs and projects or as a strategic and visionary resource?

This is *not* going to be about whipping yourself into shape, answering long questionnaires, or taking a happy pill and everything will be all right with the world. It's about being quiet for a bit. Thinking about yourself. Reflecting on the things you have and haven't done. And then moving forward with confidence and new understanding.

CHAPTER FIVE

FROM PERFECTION TO PASSION

I am messy. I'm not trying to be an example. I am not trying to be perfect. I am not trying to say I have all the answers. I am not trying to say I'm right. I am just trying—trying to support what I believe in, trying to do some good in this world, trying to make some noise with my writing while also being myself.

—ROXANE GAY

The day was not what I imagined at all.

I had wanted this. The fairy tale. The romantic notion of being married in the traditionally Anglican stone church of my childhood, followed by a sumptuous sit-down dinner served in a golden-lit marquee (or tent) in my parents' garden, with dancing and drinks around the pool.

Instead, we had a home full of harried relatives too nervous to leave for the church in case any severe damage was caused by the approaching storm, an electrical circuit board that consistently could not meet the needs of an anxious caterer, and no real alternate plans to either feed or shelter the 250 invited guests.

In the midst of this general chaos, I experienced my first and only anxiety attack. So, there I was, all guipure lace and veil and makeup, rapidly breathing into a nondescript brown sandwich bag.

This bag stayed with me on the drive to the church, right up until it was time to walk down the aisle. And then my father took over:

"Okay, now," he said quietly to me. "One, two, three, breathe."

"Now, one, two, three, smile."

"Now, look to your left … and to your right."

"Good. Now, one, two, three, breathe!"

I'm sure that he was relieved to hand me over to my unsuspecting almost-husband. The rest of the service passed in a thankfully uneventful, beautiful fashion.

But the drama waited until the guests exited the church and it was time for the celebrations to begin. The heavens opened up, destroying all photo opportunities, a good portion of the marquee, and all outdoor canapé appetizer plans and making it remarkably impossible to even consider wearing shoes.

Eventually, the evening, assisted by very able bar staff and responsive barefooted guests, found its measure.

And it was then that my father stood to propose a toast to my now-husband and me. I know therapists will probably have a field day with what I am about to say, but I must admit that I was rather looking forward to this moment.

I had always wanted to be a "Daddy's little princess" type. That kind of metaphor was absent in our home. My father is supportive but not fawning. He is the kind of father who, when I was sixteen, asked me to list the five things that I aspired to. At that age, my list included things like trips to Tibet and creating rural literacy schools in South Africa, my home country. He had solemnly stored this list in our household safe to emphasize the importance of the document. So, wonderful man, yes, and one who encouraged me to envision big possibilities for my future, but on that night—my wedding night—I wanted adoration. I wanted to hear that I was talented and bright and beautiful and much loved.

He started by talking about a trip that he had taken to Greece as a young man. He had visited the temple of the oracle at Delphi. What struck him on that trip was the well-known counsel "Know thyself," which ancient writers have recorded as being inscribed on the forecourt of the temple.

And then, looking at me, he said that when he thought of me, he thought of those words. That I had a strong sense of self, a strong sense of who I was, and having that was of tremendous value.

That was it! No lovingly sentimental stories of my childhood that illuminated my many wonderful traits. Great. I knew myself.

But, oh, how I have clung to that throughout the twenty-six years since that day. Twenty-six years of marriage. Bringing two children and innumerable pets into this world. Living and working on three different continents with shifting senses of what family and friends mean. And now, driving deep roots in a foreign country, with a world that only talks in the language of *turbulence* and not merely *change*. What do you hold on to? What guides each choice, each direction, and helps you deal with each twist or drama? It is that very sense of self.

A sense of knowing where you come from and what is important to you; a sense of which skills and knowledge and interpersonal style—your character—you bring to personal and professional settings; a sense of your aspirations and imaginations of what you hope for yourself personally and for your family. That's what makes the decisions easier; that's what gives you the confidence when things feel a bit shaky and the strength when you feel very foreign and alone.

And it's that very sense of self that eludes so many of the clients I work with. That's why I share this story. Almost on a daily basis, I am reminded of the value of one's identity (and reminded that all women should carry emergency brown paper sandwich bags).

I work predominantly with women at different points and stages in their lives and careers—from women in tremendous positions of corporate leadership, to successful business owners, to women in transition, whether that means reentry to the workplace or to a second career. And with all of these women, I keep hearing the same language. Regardless of where these women find themselves, they speak about how overwhelmed and ungrounded they feel—overwhelmed by the daily grind of what they do and what needs to be done. They talk of feeling that their lives are out of control; they share that they feel sad, unhappy, frustrated, lost. They do not have a moment for themselves and no time for any creative outlets. There is often a profound sense of isolation, of not being understood, of standing alone. This is a place where, as one client put it—and it's very violent imagery—she feels stuck in a sausage machine: torn apart, shredded, churning, and just hoping that she will pop out the other side in one piece!

It seems that, at some level, we could all use some kind of breathing assistance.

But for me, the question really is why? Why do we end up in this place?

My sense is that, as women, many of us seem to have this near-reflexive tendency to get lost in the perfect, in being everything to everybody. It's that wild want, that obsession, to be the *perfect* leader ... the *perfect* mother ... the *perfect* spouse or *perfect* friend ... the *perfect* executive, *perfect* community leader, *perfect* host. And the perfect list goes on and on and on.

And what happens then is that, rather than discovering our potential, we actually dismiss, discount, and diminish the very power, perspectives, and possibilities that we have in hand. We overlook and underappreciate who we already are and what's already in play.

This is what I mean by getting lost. We cover over what's personally meaningful to us. By setting up perfection as the goal, we ultimately end up questioning our value, our worth, our talents, and, finally, our very identity.

And even as I say this, I am nervous, because you, like all of the highly accomplished, fabulous women I am referring to, are probably at a very deep level proud—proud of being perfect. It's okay. It's no secret. Our culture values and reinforces the notion of perfection and with it the sense that if we are not being perfect, we are slacking off at some level. We take pride in being perfect, but do you ever think that maybe we have missed the point?

CLIMBING THE SPIRAL STAIRCASE

I also recognize that I am writing this from a position of privilege. My story is not yours. Because of your race, your gender, your cultural background, the pressures to be "perfect" will be different and will feel different. Perhaps your "perfect" involves the way you present yourself to the world. Perhaps it involves your ability to code-switch. Perhaps it involves the identity you feel comfortable claiming—and the one that truly resonates inside you. Perhaps it involves the emotions you feel safe expressing and those you keep bottled up inside.

> **We take pride in being perfect, but do you ever think that maybe we have missed the point?**

Still, I am convinced that this persistent drive toward perfection universally hurts us. And, of course, I also am confident that there is another way to be—an alternative. This chapter is about making that shift. We will explore how you can transition from being lost in perfect to living in passion. Passion is something much more valuable than perfection. Please, have the absolute assurance from me that this is not about slacking off—this is not about mediocrity.

I have two absolute beliefs. The first is that we all aspire to be somebody of which we can be proud. The second is that we all want to be part of something bigger than ourselves. When we can achieve those two, when we can live our aspiration, then we live from a place of passion.

LOST IN TRANSITION

Let me share some examples of what "lost in perfect" looks like in my world.

First, I'll share an email I received from a coaching client. She was working through a process I had designed for her on her leadership story. For homework, I had asked that she take a "snapshot" of who she was at the moment—her skills, her concerns, the things that were important to her and her style, the way she does the things she does. And this is what I heard back:

Hi Leanne,

When I came to "catch a glimpse of myself" in the story—I couldn't! I couldn't find myself anywhere ... even in the narrative of my life, the details of my life. I am beginning to wonder if I have lived my life so much doing things that have not really been an expression of my individual self, but rather doing things to minimize the risk of rejection, that I have lost sight of myself.

So, now I am a little stuck—how do you go on to plot your personal narrative when you are not in it? How do you find even a glimpse of yourself in a life that seems to have been lived by someone playing you? If I didn't have a sense of humor, this would be quite scary. Or have I just done the exercises incorrectly and misunderstood the instructions?

What is your reaction when you read this email? Do you resonate with her sense of somehow being missing from her own story?

If so, please know that this experience is not dissimilar to the many I hear from my coaching clients. I work with unbelievably talented, competent, successful women in all walks of life who see none of the light they bring to workplaces. Like the client who sent this email, many seem at a crossroads, stuck in jobs for which they have lost their passion, unable to strike a balance among their varied roles and interests, yet at a loss for a better alternative. They talk about the fact that something seems to be missing, yet they don't know what that is or what change they would like to make or how to move forward.

Then there are the successful women business owners who have built wealth and employment for many and support for their families, and now they feel trapped and isolated. Trapped, in some cases, by the fact that what they are doing no longer gives them any meaning yet knowing that many people are dependent on them for their livelihood.

Do you find yourself lost in this transition point? Are you a woman who has spent years being the perfect boss, the tough businesswoman, attentive to clients' needs, the optimist, the cheerleader, the mothering hen to staff and her own family, and now, you lift your head up to see … nothing. No clear understanding of who you are, separate from your role in your company or your role in meeting the requirements of your aging parents and grown children. No clear understanding of what you would like to do moving forward but with a deep sadness for what you may have lost of yourself along the way.

This message extends beyond women caught up in their careers. Maybe you don't have a traditional career or job. But that doesn't make the sense of being lost in the perfect any easier! None of us seem to get off lightly. The stats on stay-at-home moms and depression are pretty gloomy. According to a Gallup poll of more than sixty thousand US women, nonemployed moms of young children are more likely to report anger and sadness, and they are also more likely to have been diagnosed with depression than their employed counterparts.[36]

And yes, I have been there. I shared with you in chapter 2 my time in the nugget-strewn kitchens with other hardened veterans of suburbia as we poured our first drink at 4:00 p.m. to "take the edge

---

36 Elizabeth Mendes, Lydia Saad, and Kyley McGeeney, "Stay-at-Home Moms Report More Depression, Sadness, Anger," Gallup, May 18, 2012, https://news.gallup.com/poll/154685/stay-home-moms-report-depression-sadness-anger.aspx.

off." Finding the quiet and uninterrupted space or time to think or be yourself outside of being someone's mom, someone's spouse, the good neighbor, and the diligent PTA member can present quite the struggle.

When I stayed home, I found it hard to even have perspective on my kids' lives, never mind the challenge of contemplating my own. I would go so far as to say that my self-esteem became ridiculously linked to my children's. They would have a tough day, and it would hurt me terribly, followed by the nagging questions of how I must have failed to prepare them at some level for whatever that day presented.

And then there were anxiety-inducing conversations with the glam gals—friends who not only managed to look gorgeous in this domestic mayhem but also seemed to stay on top of the schedules and know the best teachers to ask for and coaches to find, all while perfecting their tennis form and maintaining a French manicure.

The secret clubs of mothers were just as intimidating. They loved being pregnant, remembered every developmental milestone of each child, and literally glowed while preparing only homemade organic meals for their offspring.

We all have our stories of how and where we've focused on the misleading goal of trying to be "perfect." Many involve stories of individuals and groups of women, but my work with organizations and institutions provides equally telling stories.

Many organizations are interested in our university's executive education programs, as they have come to the clear understanding that women professionals face a distinct set of challenges and are motivated by a more complex series of career goals than those of men. They recognize that a one-size-fits-all general notion of executive development no longer seems that effective.

I also work with corporations that have tried hard to create inclusive work environments so that women employees would thrive, but now, instead of talking about the glass ceiling, they talk about the "sticky floor."

What is that sticky floor? It's the understanding that something—beyond making sure that processes like recruitment, development, and succession plans are equitable—stands in the way of women's progression in organizations.

This "something," this missing piece, has to do with our identity. How we, as women, understand ourselves and then bring who we are into the settings in which we work and play.

Let me be clear: I'm not suggesting that the onus is purely—or even largely—on women. There are structural issues that should and must change for real equity, and there is important work to be done on how we de-bias our systems.

But in this book, I want to empower you as an actor within those existing structures. I want to challenge you to ask yourself fundamental questions—questions like "What is holding me back? What is keeping me from stepping up and stepping into important opportunities?"

Later in this book, we'll talk about fear of failure and fear of success. But pause here, just for a moment, and ask yourself that question: "What is holding me back?"

Your response might be: "I need to meet my family's requirements right now." "I need to provide for my children." I need to … I need to … I need to … in a long list of explanations.

Too often, we allow these explanations, and the desire to meet the needs of others, to excuse us from stepping into who we *could* be.

In a recent conversation with the executive director of a national association of women MBAs, we discussed her concern that, after reviewing the results of their annual survey, she saw that women MBAs who were five to seven years into their careers were losing confidence. She attributed this directly to a lack of sense of self—a feeling that who they are as a person, beyond what they deliver, is not valued or defined in their organization.

This notion of being valued for what we do, and not who we are, goes to the heart of being "lost in perfect." For a number of reasons (which we'll dive into in a moment), we as women seem to have this overwhelming need—in Afrikaans, we would use the word *drang*, a strong impulse—to be everything to everyone, to be perfect at all that we do.

But the problem with this is that the neglected parts of who we are eventually come back to haunt us. And they come back as depression, burnout, and frustration, the increasing sense of injustice, or the *overwhelmedness* that I alluded to earlier.

So, it's not just the biases of our systems—the glass ceiling—that can limit our leadership journey. Sometimes there are things we need to release, expectations to let go of, to be more effective and to move forward.

THE IMPERFECT PERFECT

Are you a little angry? Emotional? Disappointed? Scared? Feeling alienated? Or not able to really answer, for all the white noise in your head?

You are not alone.

In her 2009 article "Blue Is the New Black," Maureen Dowd notes that "women are getting gloomier," pointing to the results of the General Social Survey, which has tracked Americans' moods since 1972, and other major studies around the world.[37]

---

37 Maureen Dowd, "Blue Is the New Black," *New York Times*, September 19, 2009, www.nytimes.com/2009/09/20/opinion/20dowd.html.

Arianna Huffington validates this further in her article published that same year, "The Sad, Shocking Truth about How Women Are Feeling," in which she notes that women have made gains in so many arenas yet, in her words, "women around the world are in a funk."[38]

More than a decade later, very little has changed. In fact, the coronavirus pandemic has increased pressure on working women—and added to their sense of being overwhelmed by responsibilities for others. A 2020 report published by McKinsey on women in the workplace reveals that one in four women were considering leaving the workforce or downshifting their careers because of COVID-19. Companies are at risk of losing up to two million women, wiping out much of the gains women have made in management levels over the last few years.[39]

Elizabeth Perle McKenna's seminal book, *When Work Doesn't Work Anymore*, contains many illuminating indicators, including the following numbers from a Fortune and Yankelovitch survey of female managers and executives:[40]

- Eighty-seven percent of the women surveyed wanted to make a major change in their lives.

- Forty percent felt trapped.

- Sixty percent were in therapy.

Interestingly, though, self-confidence wasn't the problem: 81 percent responded that they were better at their jobs than most men. The glass ceiling wasn't the problem: between 65 percent and 78 percent were expecting to make significant advances in the near future.

---

38 Arianna Huffington, "The Sad, Shocking Truth about How Women Are Feeling," HuffPost, November 17, 2009, https://www.huffpost.com/entry/the-sad-shocking-truth-ab_b_290021.

39 McKinsey & Company and Lean In, *Women in the Workplace 2020*.

40 Elizabeth Perle McKenna, *When Work Doesn't Work Anymore: Women, Work, and Identity* (New York: Delta, 1997), 2.

But even more to the point: "Three quarters of the women surveyed felt that they were defined and valued by what they did and not who they are."[41]

My sense is that women have become so adept at meeting the requirements of others that they have lost a sense of who they are. Strong women, powerful women, women in positions of leadership, as indicated in these surveys, have fallen prey to this. They have met these requirements and are well rewarded for it, but in this process, they have lost a sense of who they are. In a society that rewards women for meeting others' requirements rather than their own, it's easy to lose our sense of who we are.

And sadly, this feeling of being lost in perfect is not only the purview of grown women. A recent study published by the organization Girls Inc. described not a super*woman* dilemma but rather a super*girl* dilemma.[42] Girls today experience intense pressure at ever-younger ages to be everything to everyone. They are feeling pressure to be perfect, accomplished, thin, and accommodating.

I was surprised to find that even young men seem to be well versed in this notion of "effortless perfection." At a corporate seminar I was facilitating, a few male graduates from Duke University explained a memorable debate while they were still students that arose from a study on the status of women at the school.

This study found that "many of Duke's undergraduate women were entering the university with a great deal of self-confidence, but were graduating four years later with eating disorders, stress-related illnesses, and an overall sense of insecurity and self-doubt."[43]

---

41   McKenna, *When Work Doesn't Work Anymore*, 3

42   Girls Inc., *The Supergirl Dilemma: Girls Grapple with the Mounting Pressures of Expectations* (New York: Girls Incorporated, 2006).

43   VOA News, "Freshman Women at Duke University Battle 'Effortless Perfection,'" October 29, 2009, www.voanews.com/archive/freshman-women-duke-university-battle-effortless-perfection.

As Donna Lisker, the then-director of the Duke Women's Center, explained, women felt compelled to "be not only academically successful, but also successful by all the traditionally female markers—thin, pretty, well-dressed, nice hair, nice nails. And, the real rub is you had to do it with no visible effort."[44] Effortless perfection.

You may well be shaking your head in horror. This is not you. Not your daughter. Not the women in your life. You still are not sure what I mean by this "lost in perfect thing."

So, before moving on, let's do one last "perfect check."

Think of your last holiday meal. It can be any celebration that is important to you. Thanksgiving is one of my favorite adopted holidays. But it could be Christmas dinner, Passover Seder, an Eid al-Fitr feast, or a special meal for your Diwali party. You get the picture.

Almost every woman I speak with has, at one time or other, gone out of her mind trying to make a holiday meal—to create a perfect day. The stories are wonderful, from manically carved turkey-shaped butterballs to 4:00 a.m. tears falling on red bows tied around dinner rolls. The table is set two days in advance. Plans are made for a seven-course meal, perfectly timed, and presented with a Balanchine grace. When something goes the least bit wrong—say, the wine wasn't decanted properly or the napkins were forgotten—the whole experience is "ruined."

By demanding perfection, we find ourselves facing abstraction, frustration, isolation, and failure.

And so, if you are tired of this—tired of being overwhelmed, feeling lost, waking up with a shaky feeling in the pit of your stomach—then let's walk together awhile. Let's lose perfect and relax into the presence of who you are. Let the passion of who you are trump perfect.

Rather than seeing, chasing, earning validation and approval from others by doing the "right thing" and by following the rules (which, if

---

44   VOA News, "Freshman Women at Duke University Battle 'Effortless Perfection.'"

you think about it, is inherently passive, submissive, and oppressive), let's focus on sensing what's important and precious.

To live from a place of passion is to live from a place deep within yourself. There's no need to go outside to find it or to work hard to achieve it. It's already here waiting to emerge. It's about looking inside and seeing your talents, your energy, your strengths, your gifts and potentialities.

> **To live from a place of passion is to live from a place deep within yourself.**

This is an opportunity to make sense of your life in a way that accounts for the past, gives hope to and for the future, and provides meaning and grounding for day-to-day living. We will be looking at ways to illuminate passions, reveal the power and import of relationships in your life, and make change and choice doable, even in the most frustrating and restricted of circumstances.

It's about reclaiming a life worth living.

But if all of that sounds way too lofty right now, I would advise you to go and buy that brown sandwich bag. Keep it on hand at all times. And when that perfect list gets too long, just breathe.

"In, two, three."

"Out, two, three."

Feeling better? Good. Now, I have a request. I want you to pause here and think of just one thing you are going to let go of.

It's really as simple as that. No big plans. No to-do lists.

Just a question: What one perfect thing are you going to let go of? Today, at this age, in this place, feeling like you are feeling.

Note the date. Today is the day you stopped being perfect about _____ . It's gone. Let it go.

WHY THIS TRANSITION MATTERS

Many of us begin each new year with fresh ambitions and goals. This is the year I'll earn that degree … apply for that opportunity … receive that promotion … start that exercise program.

And then January gives way to February, and at some point, you realize that you have given up on your ambitions and goals. Instead, you have settled. In the busyness of each day, you have forgotten to pay attention to your hopes and resolutions and intentions.

And that's a problem. We keep ourselves distracted enough so that we don't think about our goals and intentions. But every now and then, those neglected parts of who we are come back to haunt us. It's that gnawing feeling that something is not quite right. The feeling that we have not fully tapped our potential. The belief that we were put on this earth to some good purpose, and it's bigger than what we are living now. What follows, when we realize this gap between what we wanted and where we are, is often depression, frustration, or anger.

So, reason number one for contemplating this transition: At a very basic level, if you are concerned about your mental, emotional, and physical health, or if there is a longing, a stirring in you for something else, then you should bother about this. If the questioning of your life and its meaning comes up more than the annual January resolutions review of where you are and where you would be, then it's perhaps time. Time to have a look at who you are and where you are going. Time to stop losing yourself in living perfectly and move toward a passionate life.

If not now, then when? When will it make sense? Do you want to wait another year? Do you want to "settle" and do the right thing and wait until you have "everything in place?" Will you even know what it is you want to do at that stage? Will you have the confidence then to do it? Will you have the years left to enjoy it? So again, maybe now is the time.

Or maybe you can keep distracting yourself, finding all manner of good excuses for why things must remain the same. But sit in my shoes, please, for a bit. Imagine you are about to coach someone and you are sitting down opposite a talented woman you know. It could be a colleague, your mother, sister, girlfriend. Or even put yourself in the hot seat for a bit.

Now listen to this bright woman's aspirations. She has them. And listen to her reasons for why these things "cannot" happen. As she talks, you realize how easily she is distracted by other people's needs. She is responsible for this person and that kid, this parent and that partner. The list goes on. And yet you still hear the yearning for something more, something different.

So, you push harder, and you hear about fear. Fear of not getting it right, not having the skills. As articulate and composed as she may seem, you realize that there is a deep lack of confidence. What if she fails and there is no one to blame? What excuse will she use? You wonder, what is easier? Not to do it? To say you can't because your kids need you, your parents need you, your colleagues and clients need you?

We pride ourselves on being go-to people. Proactive, strong people. Yet at our core, we do not feel we are worthy. And, in fact, we are maybe a little wimpy. We do not feel that we could pull this off. So, we stay hidden behind the requirements of perfect. We do things perfectly, which is safe and impressive, and allow ourselves every now and then to feel a bit sorry for ourselves, a bit victimy. We settle.

But what if there was a different way to live? When was the last time you felt enthusiastic? Enthusiastic comes from the Greek word *enthusiasmos*. It's a concept that I am very taken with and that means "filled with the gods." It's about a state of ecstasy when the individual loses all sense of their normal self and gains a glimpse of their immortal self.

Imagine if you had that to draw on. Your own reserves of energy, ideas, and inspiration.

It's been done before. Just look around you. You will see the people who have chosen this path. They are enthusiastic. No, everything is not easy and bad things still happen, but when you are engaged and enthused, you have reserves—energy and strength to draw on to deal with whatever comes along. At your core, you are stabilized by a clear understanding of who you are and what you want and which direction you are moving in, and so the demands and the crises and the requests are dealt with from a place of strength instead of a place of weakness, where the slightest setback creates a sense of being completely overwhelmed.

You already have this. You have everything at hand to live this way, to make it happen. Now is the time to stand in your light.

The writer Anna Quindlen says, "Nothing important, or meaningful, or beautiful, or interesting, or great, ever came out of imitations."[45] And it's this notion of imitation that takes me to my second reason for why you should bother taking the time now to live the life to which you aspire. Perhaps, for some of you, the whole preceding section was a bit heady; perhaps you have no real need or yearning for something different.

So, let's look to economics for reason number two of why you should shift from a life built around a list of requirements to one filled with meaning.

---

45 Anna Quindlen, "Commencement Speech" (Speech, Mt. Holyoke College, South Hadley, MA, May 23, 1999).

MOVING THE WORLD

In merely meeting the requirements of a situation, no matter how perfectly you meet them, you are offering nothing more than imitation. You may be confusing perfection with competence and, in this process, losing your very competitive advantage.

In a global, highly competitive world where people can be sourced and replaced from anywhere, I believe our uniqueness is our only true asset. Think about the hiring process. Often, what wins the day is an individual's unique spark—that something extra that distinguishes a person or group. It's their take on something that is of interest. That is what is going to excite recruiters, not a candidate's functional competence. Competence is essential, but in my mind, it has almost become a minimum requirement. Competence is what gets the job done, but it does not add the value that you, your family, or your clients need.

I work with a distinguished school district. At the beginning of each year, they receive four thousand applicants for open positions within their district. That's four thousand people, all with a minimum of a master's degree, from good education programs, vying for a handful of jobs. So, how do you pick the math teacher?

Yes, you look at the qualifications and the experience, but what you are interested in is the *enthusiasmos*—the spirit within them, what they uniquely bring. Their ideas, their opinions, their aspirations, their energy, their thinking, the way they execute, how they uniquely take up their role.

That's job security. You take those things wherever you are. And when you become appreciated for who you are, not just what you do, that's a competitive and confident place to be.

There's one more reason why this transition point matters. It involves influence—moving the world.

If you aspire to any form of leadership—thought leadership, corporate leadership, leadership in your community—you need clarity on who you are. Strong leaders have strong stories; they have a strong sense of where they came from, of who they are now and what they imagine for the future. That's what we follow. If you are meeting requirements, you are nothing more than a competent worker, not a leader. We follow people because of who they are, what they believe, the vision they have. We do not follow those who merely execute tasks well. We appreciate them, but we do not value and respect them as leaders.

If you are on a quest to develop as a leader, the very first step is an inner pursuit to discover who you are—your passion or passions. It's through this process of self-examination that you will find the awareness needed to lead. If you are lost in perfect, with no idea of who you are separate from meeting the requirements of a situation, with no clear understanding of what you personally and uniquely bring to situations, then it will be impossible to achieve the inspirational leadership—the leading with heart—that we know is essential for influence.

WHY PERFECTION?

If you are now contemplating or are committed to transitioning from a life built around notions of perfection to one that embraces passion, then it is important to know why you get lost in perfect in the first place.

Think back to the concepts we discussed earlier. Nurture and nature and gender. Locus of control. Cultural factors. If we are going to make this shift from perfection to passion, shifting from being lost in merely meeting the requirements of a situation to instead living from a place that reflects who we are and what we aspire to, then we need to have clarity on our identity, an understanding of the things that shaped who we are today. We need to have our eyes wide open to the influences of our milieu, our gender, and our very nature. These are the things that shape our beliefs, practices, and ideas.

Quite frankly, when I look around me, in the environments in which I work and play, I am not seeing many men struggle with being "lost in perfect." And I know I am making vast generalizations. And I know that we all have unique blends of masculine and feminine qualities.

But too often, the women I coach are willing to—without realizing it—place themselves in a secondary position. Maybe this has happened to you. You try so hard to meet the requirements of others, whether real or imagined. Enough is rarely good enough. You always feel that you could have done or should have done more. You get lost in always wanting to be seen in a positive light—the ideal friend, the sleek body, the seductive love, the engaged neighbor, the stellar boss. You spend too much time trying to prove your value and worth to others—an endless, identity-dissolving cycle of chasing perfection.

As women, we have been socialized to be relationship oriented. Please don't misunderstand. This relational orientation is an asset in the workplace, where collaboration, teamwork, cooperation, social skills, and mentoring all matter. These are skills that are highly sought after and valued.

But equally we need to understand that there is a shadow side to our relational identity. Although we live and find meaning in relationships, too often we become abstracted from the relationship by getting caught up in the perceived needs, requirements, and expectations of the people we are in a relationship with. And here is the danger, for this is where and why we lose ourselves in the perfect, where we try to be everything to everyone.

Think of how many people you come in contact with in one day—both in person and virtually—and how many relationships are involved.

From the time you wake your family up and get them ready for the day, to your colleagues at work and their deadlines, to a client who isn't satisfied with a presentation, and on and on. So many opportunities to get lost in the perfect. To get lost in meeting the requirements of what you think the role is for that moment: competent boss, compassionate daughter, invested employee. Instead of acting purely from a place of strength, the strength of knowing and choosing and deciding and saying things because this is who you are and how you would choose to respond—a place where your actions in your relationships reflect who and what you are—you focus on merely meeting the requirements of a situation, reacting in the moment. That's when the to-do list becomes too long and the daily grind exhausting.

So how do you do it? How do you transition from the exhaustion of filling a role, playing a part, being perfect to fully living and working with passion and energy?

PASSION THREADS

At the beginning of this book, I encouraged you to identify your passion token—the object that will help you see, remember, and connect to the aspirations and imaginations of who you are when you are at your best.

I hope that you identified your passion token. I hope that you keep it close at hand. Because the emotion you experience through your token—emotion that helps you remember your goals for a life rich with meaning—leads to an important point.

While women have no real problem identifying all of the things that give them meaning, it is a real struggle to remember what those things are in our daily living. And it's even more difficult to build a life where we live to the best of who we are in relationship with others doing the things we care about in a fashion that is congruent with what we uniquely bring to this world.

That is precisely why I'm urging you to make this transition—the transition to living from a place of passion as opposed to being lost in perfection. Living from a place of passion is about building a life knowing where you come from and why you do the things you do. It is about building a life where your choices and actions now reflect the future you aspire to. It's about building a life out of the things and people you love.

And this notion of "passion" is not to be confused with "purpose." So many of the women I work with have spent time attempting to discern their "one unique purpose." They believe that if they can just solve that puzzle, then their lives would magically fall into place. Work, career, place, and people would all come together to serve that unique purpose.

The problem with this is that we are always looking for potential, always looking for something outside ourselves. Always looking to become something *other*. Waiting. Discerning. Who we are and the present we live in are continually deficient at some level. There is always something missing. We are not complete.

But what if it's not about intercession but rather about revelation?

What if all of the ingredients for who you need to be are already here? What if it's not a matter of "stumbling" across the one way to live your life, but instead it's about building meaning into your life and allowing who you are and need to be to be revealed through your living and working?

What if your goal was to intentionally choose and commit to the people, the things, the practices, and the work that are important for how you understand yourself right now—and let the rest take care of itself?

Don't worry. There are themes, patterns, and parts of who you need to be that will not let go of you. If you look at your life over time, there are identity-defining unique skills that have come a long way with you. The way you do the things you do, your character, your passion—they are all right there from the beginning.

Don't believe me? Go back to your nursery school or early childhood assessments. In our family, these documents have been the staple fodder for each milestone speech that needs to be made. Graduation? Marriage? Rite of passage? My parents rip out those old pieces of paper and explain to everyone that the key ingredient was there all along.

Remember my story at the beginning of this chapter, in which my father praised me for my strong sense of self?

This is my nursery school report:

> *Leanne does not mix much with the other children and can be very solitary at times, but this seems to be from choice.... Leanne is a popular member of her group, but she seems to hold herself aloof at times, preferring the company of the older girls ... most interested in stories.... She uses her imagination and can at times work very well and carefully ... there are times, however, when she seems to need to mess, then her creative work can be very careless and untidy.*

I suspect that you'll find something similar as you look back and reflect—threads that illuminate and make sense of the path you are already on. If there is no well-documented paper trail of your development, and you would like to catch sight of what I call "passion threads," then ask eight to ten people whose opinions and insights you trust and value for feedback on the passions, qualities, traits, and abilities they appreciate in you or find of value. It can be fun to include someone who knew you when you were young—a teacher or neighbor—to find those early hints of the person you were already fully becoming.

To live from a place of passion is not to say, "How do I define my one purpose and go and follow that?" Instead, it's this: "Given what is important to me, how do I live more into each of those areas? How do I build a life where I exercise my skills at work in a way that I find engaging?" The more you answer these questions, the more you live into your passions, the more robust a life you will enjoy, and the greater clarity you will experience moving forward.

It begins by knowing what is important to you. Your passions. It's not what someone else said should be important to you or what you have been socialized to believe is important. Instead, it's a keen understanding of what gives you meaning—what excites you, or sustains you, or that which you love. It's about the *enthusiasmos* I spoke of earlier—the alive joy or engagement where you feel connected and part of something bigger than yourself.

The more you live to that, to the things that give you this meaning, the closer you are to who you need to be. The more you align yourself with your most natural state of being, the closer you are to that very "purpose" you may be looking for. And quite frankly, the greater your chance of simple peacefulness—of getting through a day with a sense of accomplishment or joy or satisfied fullness.

At a base level you probably believe that you are either here to love or to redeem or to heal or to do great works. Why not think about that as your broad purpose? How you do this, how you live out this purpose, is through your passions. How you uniquely take up this purpose is to build a life combining these passion ingredients into a unique pattern that will be your life—a life that has dignity and meaning for you. Passion and purpose.

To live passionately does not mean you have to walk away from everything in your life and go and write that book or travel through the Sinai Desert or work with the Sisters of Mercy. So often, women come to me for coaching because they are dissatisfied with their work and are looking for a solution. At the same time, they are a little nervous that, in looking at their life, we are going to come to the conclusion that they have to give up everything they have worked so hard for. And so I remind them first that they are going to come to their own insights—I am not in the business of providing an antidote—and second, that "solutions" are more nuanced than we imagine. Life and its commitments come in subtle shades of gray. Meaning and sense-making are more often than not circular, iterative processes where, in the different seasons of our lives and growth, different things make sense at different times.

One of my clients is a woman named Billie, a product of "hippy parenting—wonderful love but absolutely no structure." Billie promised herself that she would configure her own family differently one day. And she does by providing parameters and organization and routine. As she has married into a traditional Italian family, the evening meal is a fixture on a schedule she likes to keep. The only problem? She has little interest in thinking about food, buying food, cooking food, or, for that matter, discussing it.

Dinner had become this awful burden, weighing down the edges of her day. Only when she takes two steps back does she realize that, for her, the meal is not about food at all. In fact, she could bring in food or use the offered cooking support of many relatives or services that are available. For Billie, the evening meal keeps the rhythm of the day, honors what is important to her husband, and allows her to experience the warmth of her relationships with her family members. It is not about whether she cooks or not.

Sound silly? I think not. There is so much to do in each day, and it's so easy, in the name of efficiency, to fall into patterns of acting and behaving and thinking. For a long time in my early career, I worked on "revolutionary thinking" training where we would ask clients to list the five things they hated about their jobs. We would then take each item and ask, "Why did this activity, program, concept, project, or idea come to be?" And then the follow-up question, "Do these reasons still exist?"

Most clients never knew the reasons for why they did what they did, never mind whether those reasons were still valid or not. No wonder so many organizations struggle to remain relevant.

Knowing why and for what reasons you do things places work, career, and living in an integrated context. Knowing the larger context, you then can see what meaning you get from work and how your skills, talents, and abilities are applied in ways that do or don't promote your sense of identity.

If we want to identify, obtain, and succeed in work that we can take pride in and that contributes to a fulfilling identity, we need to be clear where the meaning is, where the passion is.

For many of us, work is a large part of how we understand ourselves. We work to exercise skills we enjoy and to create an identity of which we can be proud. Work is, or ought to be, something that offers a significant degree of intrinsic gratification. At its best, work—whether building a better mousetrap or finding a cure for a dreadful disease—can be a satisfying project that involves important relationships and core values. We are motivated as much by meaning in our work as we are by money or status.

So, where is the meaning in your work? Is it from your income? Is it from friendships with colleagues, or using your project management skills for a new product initiative, or being the person who can create order out of chaotic departments, or the kick you get from flexing your new leadership skills?

This sense of clarity and purpose, of knowing why you do the things you do, provides a solid grounding to engage in work with vigor and intent. From this place, you can lead, mentor, support others, and champion causes with strength. This results in a confidence and constancy of intention.

Ultimately, the payoff is that, when you come to live in passion, in meaning, you find lucidity. In a sense, you quit looking for potential and allow it to reveal itself through your living and working. You become steadfast. You tend to be less distracted by the ancillary, the unimportant, and the false tease of perfection. You become more flexible and responsive.

If you realize you have a passion for "silence," you can make sure that you build quiet practices into your days, and you understand why, in the past, some environments had you on edge. Instead of thinking that there is something wrong with you, you aren't being a perfect houseguest or committee member or you are antisocial, you realize that the noise and the constant busyness are not your thing. Or, if you have a passion for "engaging people searching for purpose," you understand for the first time that it really is no surprise that whether you are next to a sports field or in the grocery store, waiting for a flight or a haircut, you always seem to attract the person who needs to discuss their next step.

Passion is knowing what is meaningful. Passion is the antidote to perfection.

Passion is not compartmentalized. Our lives are not neatly configured into boxes. Work, home, social, spiritual, and communal are all intertwined and ever present, and our passions, the things that are important to us, are woven across this tapestry.

My challenge to you is to begin to answer this question: What is meaningful to you? What matters?

Right here and now, be quiet. Listen to your response.

If you feel anxious, if you are struggling to find your answer, remember: one, two, three, breathe.

Reflection Points

1. What one "perfect" thing have you committed to let go of?

    _____

    _____

    _____

    _____

    _____

2. When was the last time you felt a sense of *enthusiasmos*?

    _____

    _____

    _____

    _____

    _____

3. Which passion threads inform the pattern of who you need to be ?

_____

_____

_____

_____

_____

CHAPTER SIX

FROM CLUELESS TO CONNECTED

Network smarter, not smarmier.

—PROFESSOR BRANDY AVEN

A s you advance in your career, you may discover a growing mismatch between the competencies that helped get you where you are and the competencies you will need to continue to progress. Early in your career, your technical competencies were usually sufficient. Your primary responsibility was to perform specific tasks—for example, in sales, engineering, financial analysis, or work on consulting projects. Your success was based principally on your individual expertise, actions, and contributions. Even in your first managerial position, excellent technical competencies were probably sufficient.

But, as you continue to progress, technical competencies will not be enough. Your success will depend more and more on your human competencies—your ability to do the important interpersonal work of developing effective work relationships with key individuals.

Earlier in the book, I described the concept of an M-shaped career based on ebbs and flows, and it's a concept that resonates with many women I know. Women often rise very quickly early in their careers before encountering a dip—a dip that may be caused by caring for children or elderly parents.

But I think there's something equally significant to consider in these dipping points. The first arc in a career is marked by achievement. You can be successful if you hit specific goals. But in the second arc of your career, the ability to build networks of influence becomes deeply important.

The quality of your work relationships is especially critical at the upper functional and general management levels. For example, John Kotter, in a seminal study of general managers, found that one of the factors that distinguished those general managers with consistently outstanding performance records from their counterparts was their ability to develop and maintain a strong network of relationships.[46]

Managers are enmeshed in a web of relationships with people who make what often seem like unending, often ambiguous, demands. Their job is to reconcile others' numerous and conflicting expectations by developing an *agenda*, a framework within which they can make strategic decisions to commit their team to significant courses of action. As the formal authority and the nerve center for their teams, managers are uniquely placed to balance and manage inevitable trade-offs and to equitably negotiate and integrate their team's interests with those of others. Managers can implement their agendas only by effective *network building* with a complex set of people both inside and outside the organization. Managers rely on their networks not only

---

46   John P. Kotter, "What Effective General Managers Really Do," *Harvard Business Review*, March-April 1999, https://hbr.org/1999/03/what-effective-general-managers-really-do.

to get things done on the job in the short and long term but also to develop both personally and professionally and to get ahead.

It's this point—the action of engaging in effective network building—that forms the heart of the next transition I want to equip you to understand. How do you transition from being a rock star at work to having a meaningful impact on the organization? How do you move from being an expert to being an achiever?

To become a meaningful leader in your organization, your career progression must become more about driving strategic results by effectively managing others and building networks of influence and less about individual performance. This is a critical inflection point when you, as an aspiring leader, must change your perspective on what is important. That means you'll also have to consider how you prioritize and how you spend your time.

Let's pause for a moment here while you answer this question: How important is having a good network to your ability to accomplish your goals?

Too often, we confine active networking to specific points in our career: for a young person starting out, trying to find a job; for a more established professional who needs access to certain markets. But the reality is that your network is vital at all stages of your career.

Your network can also bring you joy. Your professional connections can sometimes lead to meaningful friendships.

The relationships in your network hold the key to your current capacity and future success. It's not a surprise, I'm sure,

> **The relationships in your network hold the key to your current capacity and future success.**

to recognize that networking is important. But if you think about networking as unpleasant or transactional—the image of the happy hour where you're studying name tags, trying to identify who you *should* be talking to—then I want you to also recognize that your attitude toward networking may be limiting your ability to build important relationships.

Consider this quote:[47]

> *Because of their discomfort with workplace politics, women often refuse to build networks of influence, as they view this behaviour as being inauthentic and manipulative, focused on self-promotion and power grabbing. When women condemn these politics and avoid engaging, they effectively remove themselves from the game without consciously acknowledging it. They spend all their time carrying out the content of their job. Smart employers love them for it and keep them in middle management.*

One obstacle for you may be the sense that networking is somehow dirty. It feels inauthentic. You believe that relationships should form spontaneously and organically.

Another is the belief that you'll need to invest significant amounts of time. You're so busy with achieving short-term objectives that it's challenging to step back and think more strategically.

Organizations by their nature are political environments; to succeed in them, you must learn to acquire and wield influence. I have good news: It is possible to accomplish this without power grabbing. A robust exchange of support, ideas, resources, and insights results in your team being better equipped to get the job done and you, as a leader, being better able to move beyond functional specialties and address strategic issues facing the overall business.

So, it's time for another question: What is the *quality* of your network at the moment?

---

47   Wittenberg-Cox and Maitland, *Why Women Mean Business.*

Most people build professional relationships with people who are similar to them and who are in close proximity. I don't mean to suggest that we are narcissistic or lazy, but if you look at your network and it's full of people who are very much like you, personally and professionally, then it will be challenging for you to stay current with new ideas. It will be challenging for you to *lead*.

HOW LEADERS USE NETWORKS

It can be helpful to compare how you think about your network with how leaders actually use their networks. I greatly admire the work Herminia Ibarra has done in generating greater insight into this aspect of the importance of networks. There are certain key strategies that link leadership with strategic relationship building, and it's neither inauthentic nor manipulative. Instead, Ibarra says, you can see how networking in the following ways can contribute to much more active engagement in your career:

Leaders use their networks as an essential leadership tool to equip them to

- sense trends and see opportunities;

- build ties to opinion leaders and talent in diverse areas;

- work collaboratively across boundaries to create more value;

- avoid groupthink;

- generate breakthrough ideas; and

- gather the support, feedback, and resources needed to get things done.

Can you see the possibilities? This list should help you understand how networking is much more than the awkward mixer; instead, it's about building innovative thinking and expertise.

In Ibarra's research, she explains that you have three types of networks.[48] First is the *operational network*, which contains the people at work who help you get things done. You might have a contact in IT support who you can always reach out to if you're having an issue with Zoom calls, or someone who's an expert on a specific topic who can be asked to sit in on a meeting at short notice. Next is your *personal network*—the people outside of the workplace who are kindred spirits and share your passion for specific issues and interests. Finally, the *strategic network*—the people who you can draw on to help you think about future issues and concerns. When you look ahead, these are the people you can call on to give you information about new opportunities and new directions and to help you identify future priorities.

When you think about networking, if you consider Herminia Ibarra's three categories, you can begin to understand how critical it is to look carefully at your network and begin to ask some "who" questions. Who are the people in each of your three networks? Who are your people who can help support your project? Who are your people who can provide referrals to important contacts? Who are your people who will help you identify future challenges?

If you're struggling to identify your people in these specific areas, you can sense an area—or areas?—where you may want to focus on some intentional network building. You can also see why active networking is a key leadership quality. I believe that networking is

---

48   Herminia Ibarra and Mark Lee Hunter, "How Leaders Create and Use Networks," *Harvard Business Review*, January 2007, https://hbr.org/2007/01/how-leaders-create-and-use-networks.

one of the most important things a leader does, because networking gives that leader access to resources and thinking. Your team can get things done quickly, you know who to call on for specific support and insight, and you understand the politics at play so your initiatives are more likely to proceed successfully.

I find that my clients often think of their networks too vaguely, as a broad group of contacts. It can be helpful to use Herminia Ibarra's three categories as a way to frame your thinking about your network.

AUDIT YOUR NETWORK

Let me challenge you to list ten people with whom you've discussed important work and professional matters over the past few months. You may have asked for their feedback in evaluating an opportunity, to brainstorm ideas, or for advice.

Now, take a careful look at this list. Think of this process as "performing an audit of your network." What are the strengths and weaknesses of having this set of connections at the core of your network?

Many of my clients are surprised to recognize just how small their network is. You may be, too.

You may discover some other weaknesses in your network. It may contain other women who are very much like you, limiting your access to fresh ideas, different perspectives, and future opportunities. You may have a lot of people in your social media stream, but take a look at who those people are. If they're all very much like you, then what you have is a clique, not a network.

You may discover that you're experiencing network lag—your network is all about your past, not your future. It reflects where you have been, and it doesn't contain people who can help you advance into your future goals or who represent where you are going.

Another network weakness is when it contains an echo chamber. I understand—in today's world, it's comforting to live in an echo chamber where the people you're interacting with share your opinions and perspectives, but it's not helpful for your professional development. If your network consists only of people who work for your organization or your industry—there's no one outside those spheres—then it's likely that your network may be seeing you only in one specific role or specific job function. This can also lead to pigeonholing—your contacts won't be able to see you doing something different or have the connections and the knowledge to support your efforts to transition into a new role.

A strong network contains breadth, connectivity, and dynamism. It's made up of strong relationships with a diverse group of contacts across different situations. Are your relationships broad and deep enough to help support you when you hit setbacks? Do you know someone in a senior position in an industry different from yours? Do you know someone active in a political group of which you are not a member? Do you have contacts in finance, law, government, industry, education? Are you able to bridge different groups—does your network demonstrate inclusive leadership?

Does the breadth of your current network provide you with access to the resources, information, and influence you need to get things done? If not, which aspects are missing? How is your network time and energy allocated across your contacts? Are a few contacts monopolizing your time and energy? Or do you spend your time and energy more or less evenly across the people in your network? Can you mobilize the resources you need to move your initiatives forward? If not, which relationships should be strengthened? Finally, do your ties evolve as you evolve—or is your network the same people, discussing the same issues?

I'm going to challenge you here to perform a network diagnosis. Do you see patterns and preferences? Is your network all female? All from similar backgrounds to yours? Does your network contain people from different professions, different races, different industries? How does this network audit reflection shape your understanding of yourself? Take a careful look and assess any gaps, given your goals.

Next, begin the process of thinking more strategically about your network. What tactics can you use to address these gaps in your network? What steps can you take to create new ties and to generate reasons for people to want to connect with you? If you're happy with your network, what should you be doing to maintain the same level of engagement—how can you keep infrequent contacts "active" so that you're not in touch only when you need a favor or have a request?

STRATEGIES FOR NETWORK DEVELOPMENT

It may be helpful to remember that network development is identity development, one of the critical aspects of establishing yourself as a leader. This involves not only coming to see yourself as a leader, internalizing a leader identity, but also having this leader identity "verified" or affirmed in a sense through your relationships with others. It's about being relationally recognized—even validated—as a leader. Your networks explicitly or implicitly give you feedback about your fit as a leader. Are you seen by your networks as a leader? Put another way, do the company you keep, your working relationships, and the professional groups to which you belong affirm and help you understand and become the leader you hope to be? If not, what needs to change? Are there specific skills and behaviors you need to be working on as part of your professional development as a leader? What changes do you potentially need to make to your networks to grow as a leader?

The good news is that there are many ways to build networks that won't require you to make cold calls, take up golf, or drink endless cups of coffee. Depending on your goals, there are tactics you can use to begin to identify people and groups who can help you learn new skills and provide career advice and support.

That's why it's so critical to identify gaps and redundancies in your network. Part of this strategic thinking involves identifying—and correcting—any areas of over- or underrepresentation. Are you missing key people or groups? Are you relying too heavily on one specific person or one core group? Do you have ties that you should be strengthening?

This kind of strategic thinking may suggest that I'm encouraging a transactional approach to networking. Not at all! Instead, I view networking as a way to be curious about the other person and to reciprocate value with value. What does this mean? Start with remembering that networking isn't "working" someone—it's building a relationship with them. You build relationships by learning about the other person and adding value to who and what they are. It's not about identifying people who can give you something; it's about building relationships where you bring value and have something to give back to the people in your network.

Let's begin with your existing network. There are some straightforward tactics you can use to keep that network strong. First, you want to manage your network and so manage your alliances. It's a kind of maintenance, using your existing strong connections to help you break into new circles. You can create links across your network and help people you are tied to develop their own networks. Remember, it's not transactional—the goal is to take advantage not of who others are and what they have to offer but of who *you* are and what *you* have to offer.

This is important work for career growth, worthy of you dedicating an hour a week or so to send emails to people, make connections, read and like posts, and share articles that you think will be of interest. It should be a habit.

When I lead workshops on building strategic networks, women consistently share how important it can be to be intentional about their network and to take the birds-eye perspective I'm recommending here as you reflect on the relationships you've grown within your network. There is also value in recognizing that you can blend professional and social networking. Your friendships are valid connections you can leverage as well. Where many women hesitate to think of their friendships as professional connections, men by and large are comfortable calling up their golf buddy or their college roommate for a favor. When you're auditing and maintaining your network, do not neglect to consider these relationships, too.

As you work to build your network, diversity should be a goal. Remember that you want a network that has breadth, connectivity, and dynamism. If you aspire to leadership, you want to ensure that your network represents a broad range of people to help you more thoughtfully engage with the interests, goals, ideas, and issues that matter to many different people. You can do this by creating relationships with others based on shared interests rather than on shared identities. Book clubs, sporting leagues, and gardening groups are all great ways to build connections based on things you're passionate about, rather than by whose office is next to yours, and it doesn't feel like work if it involves something that's of interest to you. The relationships will be much richer.

Travel to a foreign country—the context will give you an opportunity to meet people who you might not encounter at home. Intentionally expand your choice of activities to increase the possibility of meeting new people. If you love R & B music, go to the opera. If you're a passionate Republican donor, attend a Democratic fundraising event.

There's an increasing, and very welcome, focus in many organizations today on inclusive leadership and on leaders who are allies and advocates. It's vital for you to commit to building a professional network across lines of difference. It won't just happen—it must be strategic and intentional.

Do you have people of a different race from you in your network? I encouraged you to think about this in your network audit, but I'm emphasizing it again because it's important. We know that diverse networks are stronger, and yet the research shows that 75 percent of White people do not have people of color in their social network.[49]

> It's vital for you to commit to building a professional network across lines of difference.

In my own life, I realized that my network didn't represent as many diverse voices as I intended it to have, so in recent years, I've worked on addressing this issue specifically. At any meeting or conference I attend, at any gathering, I introduce myself to someone who does not look like me.

I encourage you to do the same. Challenge yourself not just to show up at gatherings but to be intentional and thoughtful in this way. Set a goal to connect with someone new—someone who doesn't look like you—and to begin to build relationships and networks that are rich and diverse. If you're in a very White or homogenous field

---

49 Allison Scott, Freada Kapor Klein, Frieda McAlear, Alexis Martin, and Sonia Koshy, *The Leaky Tech Pipeline: A Comprehensive Framework for Understanding and Addressing the Lack of Diversity across the Tech Ecosystem*, Kapor Center for Social Impact, February 28, 2018, www.kaporcenter.org/wp-content/uploads/2018/02/KC18001_report_v6.pdf.

or industry, what are you doing to make the field and your network more diverse?

There's an exercise I use with students that comes from the work of Professor Wayne Baker and his wife, Cheryl Baker, at the University of Michigan. "The reciprocity ring" is designed to help students think in new ways about how to build a network based on creating value for others. Reciprocity is the key to this—we give and we take—and it helps to ensure that relationships are built in new and interesting ways.

In a reciprocity ring, a group of you get together and you ask for things. It's an exercise built around asking for and giving help. It may be a big professional ask—"I need advice on how to get to the next level of this organization" or "I need the name of a good graphic designer to help with my project." You put out your asks and people respond. It's a way to build relationships and build diverse networks. When people feel that they can help, they will.

One member of your network may be looking for a civil engineer with project management experience. Someone else may need recommendations for a marketing group to promote a new product launch or strategies to better manage remote teams.

These are examples of professional requests, but requests can also be personal. A member of your network might want tickets to a Broadway show, or recommendations for a reliable moving company to use for a relocation, or the name of a good dentist in your town.

The key is to shift your focus from yourself—*What do I need?*—to your network—*What does this person need, and how can I help?* You may be able to help specifically with what they need—the knowledge, the information, the product, the expertise—or you may be able to offer help in the form of your contacts—someone you know has the resource or the expertise and you can facilitate that connection.

Professor Wayne Baker takes this a step further, adding that giving is not the same for everyone. "We have seen gender differences," says Baker. "Women are more likely to suffer generosity burnout. They help but don't ask for what they need, hence, burnout. Men give and ask for help." And here's where participation in the reciprocity ring can be advantageous. "In the Reciprocity Ring, participants are required to make a request. It helps when they know that everyone will make a request. Everyone is in the same boat."[50]

It's fascinating how effective a reciprocity ring is at building connections. The act of asking for or providing a favor or sharing your knowledge can ultimately be more valuable to you than the actual favor or knowledge itself. It's a way to build high-quality connections with others. It can generate positive energy—helping and being helped create positive emotions. And it's a strategic way to harness talent and resources that you were not aware of in your network. You may be astonished by what people will do to help others and amazed by the way you are able to contribute.

OVERMENTORED AND UNDERSPONSORED

When it comes to building networks of influence, I find that one of the greatest challenges for women is that they tend to be over-mentored and undersponsored. Women in companies at the moment have lots of mentors. A mentor is someone who cares about you and your career; they will help you, and some companies even allocate mentors to women. They're important sources of support, but they often tend to be older men, often men without significant power in

---

50   John Baldoni, "The Reciprocity Ring: When Giving at Work Becomes an Act Not a Check," *Forbes*, March 29, 2018, www.forbes.com/sites/johnbaldoni/2018/03/29/the-reciprocity-ring-when-giving-at-work-becomes-an-act-not-a-check.

the organization. They're good sounding boards, but they can't change the trajectory of your career.

What women need are *sponsors*. Sponsors are senior people in an organization—people with power. They can advocate for you, pulling you into meaningful projects. A sponsor is not a mentor—a sponsor is not someone whose shoulder you cry on when you experience a setback. A sponsor may be interested in your career, but that interest is generally in the context of what it means for them. Sponsors typically are more self-interested, but they also can be far more helpful when it comes to your career development.

When you think about your network, who is your sponsor in your organization? If you can't answer that question—if you can't say, "This person is my sponsor"—that is a problem that you'll want to address.

You create a relationship with a sponsor in one clear way—by consistently doing great work for them. It's not necessarily an overt relationship—you wouldn't go up to them and ask, "Do you want to be my sponsor?" However, after you've built that connection by performing well, if you learn of an opportunity, you can go to your sponsor—the person who knows you can do great work—and ask them if they're willing to vouch for you so that you can be considered. A sponsor has real power and can make something happen for you.

If you're struggling to distinguish between a sponsor and a mentor, let me add a few more details here. A mentor gives you knowledge, training, and social support. A sponsor gives you visibility, access, and power. A mentor provides feedback. A sponsor gives you access to other top executives. A mentor has interest in your career. A sponsor has power over your career.

You need both in your network. And good mentoring is particularly helpful early in your career. But as you advance, as you seek greater opportunities and, specifically, more leadership opportunities, sponsorship will be increasingly important. And so you need to invest more time in building those relationships.

I did want to highlight here how gender differences are linked to sponsorship. Men predominantly have male or mixed networks while women have mostly female networks. Given that men are more likely to hold senior leadership positions, women may end up with less access to senior-level sponsorship because of who is in their networks. The research shows that this problem is particularly acute for women of color.[51] Women, and particularly women of color, receive less support from their managers than men do. This is a problem because manager support is tied to positive outcomes like higher promotion rates and a stronger desire to stay with a company. This support translates into providing the resources needed to succeed, helping navigate organizational politics, promoting accomplishments, show-casing work, providing career advice, and advocating on their behalf for new opportunities.

To counter this, it becomes particularly important for you to think strategically about shaping a network that will give you the access you need to greater sources of support—and sponsorship.

---

51   McKinsey & Company and Lean In, *Women in the Workplace 2018*, accessed September 12, 2021, https://wiw-report.s3.amazonaws.com/Women_in_the_ Workplace_2018.pdf.

Reflection Points

1. Who would you like to connect with?

_____

_____

_____

_____

_____

2. What would you like to get from this relationship?

_____

_____

_____

_____

_____

3. Do you have expertise or resources you can share with this person?

_____

_____

_____

_____

_____

4. Are your relationships broad and deep enough to help support you when you hit setbacks?

_____

_____

_____

_____

_____

5. What areas of your network do you think may need improving to enhance your ability to move your initiatives forward? What are the two or three actions you think you could take to improve your network in these areas?

_____

_____

_____

_____

_____

6. Which are the barriers that may make it difficult for you to carry out these actions? What opportunities might help you implement these actions ?

_____

_____

_____

_____

_____

CHAPTER SEVEN

FROM WORKER BEE TO STRATEGIC RESOURCE

Women have made enormous progress on the lower and middle rungs of the career ladder, but we are failing to make the leap into senior positions. Everyone jumps to the conclusion that it's motherhood that holds women back, but often the big roadblock is the lack of executive presence—the inability to present oneself in a way that signals to the world you are leadership material.

–SYLVIA ANN HEWLETT

As I coach women in the context of these transitions, I've discovered that they unfold in evolutionary steps. For many women, the transition from perfection to passion occurs first, as you wrestle with identifying your true power, perspectives, and possibilities. As you build on that understanding, further advancement will increasingly depend on your ability to develop effective work relationships with key individuals. In this chapter, I'll focus on a transition you'll most likely need to make later in your career, as you near senior leadership levels: the transition from executor to visionary.

Perhaps you've been told that you're not "strategic." Or that you're not "leadership material." Or that you "lack executive presence."

The problem with this kind of feedback is that it's inherently biased. Too often, when we picture "executive presence," the default image for many is an older White man rather than a petite Asian woman.

While we can acknowledge that there are biases at play, it's also true that there is at least one managerial competence in which women generally score lower than men: visioning behavior.[52] Visioning behavior is most clearly demonstrated by leaders who set strategic direction, inspire others, and display a keen awareness of the opportunities and threats in their environment.

Visioning is a vital skill for leaders, and yet one of the challenges women face is the failure to recognize its importance. I've heard women dismiss visioning as a waste of time when they are busy taking care of real problems in the here and now. They don't have the patience for it. They describe it as "grandstanding" or "showboating" and assume that they can demonstrate their skills by doing specific tasks.

> Visioning is a vital skill for leaders, and yet one of the challenges women face is the failure to recognize its importance.

The bottom line is that it's not that women aren't capable of visioning behavior—they just don't view it as the critically important skill that it actually is. But people want visioning from their leaders. They want to trust that those who are leading them are able to see the big picture and understand how to move from where the organization is now to where it could and should be. And "strategic vision" is

---

52 Herminia Ibarra and Otilia Obodaru, "Women and the Vision Thing," *Harvard Business Review*, January 2009, https://hbr.org/2009/01/women-and-the-vision-thing.

considered the most critical skill boards are looking for in the future CEOs that they are hiring.[53]

Great leaders are not just effective—they are transformative.

Recently, I was working with a community of faith, facilitating a process to gain clarity on where they wanted to go with their children's ministry. There was much discussion on how to garner greater parental engagement and volunteer support for certain activities. We were all over the place in our conversation. And then someone said something that moved us in the right direction: "You cannot recruit someone to a task. You recruit someone to a vision."

So often when we are formulating plans to get from here to there, the focus turns to the activities, the steps needed to hit the target. The problem is that we often lose sight of what the end is, or in fact the end result is never really clearly defined or articulated. Instead of lifting our heads, allowing the energy that is released by a compelling vision to pull us along, we get overwhelmed or bored with the long to-do list on our calendars. We want to build a successful venture but get lost in Salesforce reminders of how many clients need contacting today. We want to be toned and healthy but cannot find motivation to get up early and get on our stationary bike. We want to build a successful children's ministry but get lost in how many programs and volunteers that will take.

This is not about lack of talent or understanding or insight. We all know capable people who fail to achieve their potential. It's about commitment. And it's difficult to sustain commitment to an activity list without a larger and clear sense of vision. So how do you stay motivated over a period of time?

---

53   Korn Ferry Institute, *Women CEOs Speak*, accessed September 12, 2021, https://engage.kornferry.com/Global/FileLib/Women_CEOs_speak/KF_Foundation_and_Drive.pdf.

In the previous chapters, you have caught glimpses of the person you want to be. You have been reminded of the things that give you meaning. You may want to take up some relationships differently. You may want to make a career transition, go back to school, learn to sew, or cycle the Youghiogheny River Trail. Or maybe you want to introduce or bring back some practices into your days that have been missing. More time for contemplation, reading, walking, prayer. But how do you do this in a sustained, integrated manner?

Being motivated for a short period of time is not very difficult. Bonuses work and so does bribery. A "buck a book" ensured that my kids read like crazy over summers. Buzz Lightyear big-boy undies were tremendously enticing during potty training days. A special event will motivate us, such as glamming up for a reunion. But how do we sustain our attempts at living differently? How do we hang in when times are tough—when hardships and obstacles feel as if they are derailing us?

My colleague and early mentor Jaco Boettger would say that you need to "work with tomorrow today." He calls this "real-time dreaming" and explains that when there is no clear and inspirational picture of the future, an individual or collective entity (think of your family or the organization you work for) will have no energy or enthusiasm. Hopelessness and helplessness will set in. People will become negative and inactive. We do not wait for the future to become despondent. We are disheartened now, in the present.

Jaco often quoted Viktor Frankl: "It is a peculiarity of man that he can only live by looking to the future … and this is his salvation in the most difficult moments of his existence."[54] As a Holocaust survivor, Frankl knew what he was talking about.

A future picture unleashes energy that pulls us along and inspires us to keep going, to make sense of the struggles or nonsense we may

---

54   Viktor E. Frankl, *Man's Search for Meaning* (Boston: Beacon Press, 2006), 73.

be dealing with currently. Instead of veering and bouncing reactively between the issues of the day, you live your life toward an overarching idea, a scheme, and a design.

Nelson Mandela painted that picture for my country, South Africa, when he spoke of a "rainbow nation." Mandela gave us hope and called us to be noble and to strive. He pulled us into a future, a future that was certainly unimaginable at a time in our history.

This is what great leaders do. Inspirational leadership in times of continuous contextual disintegration, which is our world today, should primarily focus on painting a picture of the future. Leaders today would do well to think of themselves as dream merchants, responsible for collaboratively creating and then driving visions that inspire.

Compelling visions are the only enduring way to influence, shape, and motivate performance. Anything else is shorthand.

My very first boss once explained to me that he had the members of our small department sorted out. He would use a carrot with one, a stick with another. "And me?" I asked. "I just have to give you meaningful work," was his response.

That worked for about a year and then I left. I was never quite sure how my "meaningful" work fit into the broader vision of what we were trying to achieve as a department or how any of this supported the organization's strategic vision. As I have said before, we all want to be part of something larger than ourselves, and when we tap into that, we tap into an energy and commitment that has the power to deal with the many challenges that make up living and working.

A future vision grounds us and gives us hope. Future pictures provide a context, which helps us understand why we do the things we do. We want our leaders to identify that purpose, to explain why we need to make certain choices, and to give us clarity on what our priorities should be.

Let me encourage you: There are specific strategies you can use to equip yourself for this transition into more visionary leadership. You can develop the skills you'll need. You can begin by taking steps to see the big picture of your organization—developing an understanding of how the key drivers of your business relate to each other and work together to produce profitable growth. Then you need to link this knowledge with proposals and ideas that knit this growth to the work that you do every day. Finally, and perhaps most critically, you must be able to effectively communicate this vision—your ideas—to other employees, managers, and executives. You need to become a skilled storyteller, creating and communicating a picture of what the future can be.

LEADERSHIP COMPETENCIES

Let's try an exercise, one that I use with my students. Pause for a moment and write down three or four words that your supervisor and coworkers would use to describe you. Be honest.

Now, look at your list. You may feel proud to see words like *productive* and *efficient* and *caring* on your list. But pay special attention to what may be missing. If your list doesn't contain words like *strategic, innovative, change agent,* or *visionary,* you are not demonstrating the ability to recognize new opportunities and trends in the environment and develop a strategic direction for an enterprise.

Leadership is not personal—it's not about you and what you need. It's about your stakeholders and what they need, and what they need is a vision for the future. One of the biggest developmental hurdles that aspiring leaders, male and female alike, must clear is learning to sell their ideas—their vision of the future—to numerous stakeholders. Presenting an inspiring story about the future is very different from generating a brilliant strategic analysis or crafting a logical implementation plan.

What does it mean to be "visionary"? Often, people link it to charismatic leadership, but these are different skills. Being visionary encompasses the abilities to frame the current practices as inadequate, to generate ideas for new strategies, and to communicate possibilities in inspiring ways to others.

Self-Diagnosis: Enhance Your Visionary Skills

Visionary leaders are able to sense opportunities and threats in their environment, set strategic direction, and inspire others.

Consider these three areas carefully. How well are you performing in each? Assess yourself and gather feedback. When you have identified a potential growth area, take note of the following bulleted recommendations, adapted from the Kets De Vries Institute's *Global Executive Leadership Inventory* report,[55] and begin to build the skill set you need.

1. Are you able to sense threats and opportunities in the environment? If not ...

   □ Expand your knowledge of your business—its market, its competitors.

   □ Dedicate more time to reading and research focused on your marketplace.

   □ Learn what your clients are doing.

---

55 Kets De Vries Institute, *Global Executive Leadership Inventory*, accessed September 12, 2021, www.kdvi.com/tools/16-global-executive-leadership-inventory.

2. Are you skilled at setting strategic direction? If not …

   ▫ Examine emerging customer needs and explore innovative solutions to those needs.

   ▫ Assess potential adaptations of your organization's systems and structures to better utilize existing talent and capabilities.

   ▫ Instill a culture of customer focus and innovation.

3. Are you gifted at inspiring others? If not …

   ▫ Build your communication and storytelling skills.

   ▫ Consider strategies to make the world more engaging for others.

   ▫ Manage and motivate performance in your team.

What are some examples of good strategic leadership that you've seen and can learn from? Are there any specific individuals who come to mind?

Many of the students and women I coach struggle to answer this question. It's far easier to identify visionary transformative political leaders than visionary leaders in our workplace. When I attend board meetings, when I talk to CEOs and corporate leaders, I witness far more transactional and tactical conversations than strategic visioning.

This should be an encouragement as well as a motivation. Don't beat yourself up if you've been told that you're not strategic. Recognize that few leaders are—and that's why boards have identified it as a critical skill. Companies are desperate for visionary CEOs; if you invest the time in developing this skill, you will be equipping yourself with a competitive edge as well as a key leadership asset.

The *Wall Street Journal* is delivered every day to our business school, and I encourage students to read their interviews and leadership profiles to get a glimpse of strategic visioning. You can do the same. Look for leaders who aren't simply reporting the actions they are taking but are setting them in the context of where they see the market moving in the future. They aren't afraid to move their organization in a specific and clear direction, even if they need to pivot or redirect later. Their words and actions create clarity and inform the people who work with and for them what's needed now—and tomorrow.

The way that "vision" appears in this skill set is illuminating because it's very much based on where you are focused. If your head is down—if you're buried in the weeds and just trying to get tasks accomplished—you won't be visionary. You have to consciously look up and out—far and wide—to make sense of where you are and the environment in which you are operating. You need to look up and out to assess the world around you and make judgments about it. And you need to look up and out to set a course and inspire people to move in a specific direction.

DO YOU KNOW YOUR BUSINESS?

Let's take a look at ten key questions that you should be able to answer if you want to be a strategic leader:

1. What are the top strategic priorities for your organization?

2. What are the implications for your unit or team?

3. What are some external changes or trends that impact your customer base or unit?

4. Are there any operating assumptions that may no longer be valid, given the changing external environment?

5. What is working well? What is not working well? What should your unit stop doing?

6. How would you describe the culture in your part of the organization? How does that differ from the larger organization?

7. Given the challenges and opportunities your organization is facing, what are the key competencies (skills, knowledge, abilities) that are critical for success in your organization?

8. What areas of skill development would accelerate your success within your organization?

9. How would you describe your relationship with key stakeholders (those who are critical to your success, both now and in the future)?

10. What have you done in the past year to change the competitive landscape—where have you added value through your contributions?

Spend some time considering your answers to these questions. If you want to make the transition from worker bee to strategic resource, these questions will help you identify potential growth areas that you can address.

TACTICS YOU CAN USE TODAY

Much of the important work of developing leadership competencies will take time. Knowing your business can and should be a constant process. But there are key short-term tactics I want to share with you now that will help you quickly jump-start your strategic thinking.

The first is to *schedule strategic white space*. That means building structured time into your calendar to think. With many of my clients, we build into their calendar what I call a "power hour." I encourage you to adopt this tactic yourself. Set aside one hour once a day, or once a week, to think and read, to actually work on strategy for a specific area. You may want to ask questions—a good starting point are the ten "know your business" questions I shared in the last section. You won't be able to think strategically if you have no time, so build time into your calendar to think.

The next tactic is to *enhance your delegation skills*. Too often we make the mistake of equating busyness with value or with impact. Strategic leaders understand the work that their team members could be doing, delegating to free them up to be more thoughtful about their long-term business goals and opportunities.

For many of my clients, the most challenging means to improve their delegation skills is to *manage the quality requirements of outputs instead of micromanaging processes*. Leaders do not spend significant amounts of time directing subordinates in what to do and how to do it. Instead, they set goals for outputs and specify the quality requirements. Successful leaders know how to multiply their efforts and their talents. They see delegation as a way to add value. They know that you cannot get caught in micromanagement (and essentially doing the work yourself), because if you do, you cannot increase your and your team's output. The value generated by you and your team can be increased only if you are able to "multiply" everyone's efforts to create value for the organization. The greater that multiple, the more valued you and your team will be within the organization.

What does this look like? Let me share an example from my personal life: When my boys were at home and I would return after a long day at work, I found that they had turned the kitchen upside down. Jars of peanut butter opened and left on the counter, every cabinet open, milk splattered on the floor, piles of cups and plates in the sink. So, I established new rules. My temptation was to issue specific directions: "As soon as you finish eating, I want you to make sure that the peanut butter lid is back on the jar, and this box is put back here, and you shouldn't just leave dishes stacked up in the sink, you should put them in the dishwasher, blah blah blah." But instead, I said this: "When I come home, I want a clean kitchen, and a clean kitchen means that there is nothing on the counters, the cabinet doors are closed, and the dirty dishes are in the dishwasher."

Do you see the difference? I defined the output: a clean kitchen. I specified the quality requirements: clean countertops, closed cabinets, stacked dishwasher. I resisted the impulse to micromanage the process. If my sons wanted to madly scramble to clean up two minutes before I walked in the door, if they chose to clean as they went, if they even chose not to eat anything because they didn't want to have to deal with the cleanup afterward, that was their business. I stated the desired output and the quality requirements and then allowed them to choose how best to accomplish those goals.

This is quite challenging for many of us. It's not easy to resist the temptation to micromanage the process. We may have an effective strategy, we may know which processes are the most efficient and the most likely to produce the desired results. But to be truly strategic, you need to focus on managing quality of outcome, not processes, to free up vital time.

To be effective as a strategic resource, you need to also practice the tactic of *redesigning meetings to drive performance*. How often have you found yourself in a meeting when there was no real reason for it, where the conversation spiraled down to ridiculous topics? You immediately realize that this meeting is not strategic—and the person running it is perceived in the same way. Effective meetings should be aimed at performance—agendas and goals should be based in numbers and specifics. Every meeting you run should have a preassigned duration—and should not extend beyond that time frame. The agenda should be clearly outlined. The purpose and focus should be predetermined. You want to be seen as both thoughtful and disciplined.

I've stressed the importance of communication, and in the tactical arena, one skill you can immediately begin to build is to *frame in the language of benefit*. Whenever you are communicating anything to anyone, begin to frame it in the language of how it will benefit the person with whom you are communicating. Don't spend time talking about where you are or why you've taken specific actions; instead, talk about why it matters to them. Your communication should always start with the back story—"This is the context, and this is why it's important to you." Link it to the goals that you know that they have and then revert to your pitch.

Finally, *add data last*. People think data and numbers are compelling, but I've found that stories are compelling, not numbers. Stories help you understand the context, then you can add the data. Think about your audience and then determine how to sell your story to that specific audience.

EXECUTIVE PRESENCE

We've just discussed some short-term tactical things you can do to develop visionary leadership, but now I want to spend some time discussing executive presence. I referenced it at the start of the chapter, this idea that, as potential leaders, we are being judged from a perception perspective.

I shared a quote from economist Sylvia Ann Hewlett, who has written extensively on this topic. She says that the perception of executive presence can account for as much as 28 percent of a woman's success.[56]

Clearly, this matters. You need the ability to present yourself to the world in a way that signals that you are leadership material.

I like to think of it as a kind of branding. Executive presence is connected to the brand or impression that comes to mind when people see you, hear your name, or think about you. Presence is about how you package and tell your story. It's about how you engage with others. It's about understanding how others see you.

> You need the ability to present yourself to the world in a way that signals that you are leadership material.

Hewlett identifies three pillars of executive presence:[57]

- *Gravitas*: The ability to project confidence, poise under pressure, and decisiveness

- *Communication*: Excellent speaking skills, assertiveness, and the ability to read an audience or situation

- *Appearance*: Looking polished and pulled together

Too often, given faulty messaging in the media and vague feedback, women make the mistake of assuming that executive presence is only connected to the third of Hewlett's pillars—appearance. But it's much more than the shade of lipstick you use or the type of suit you are wearing—in fact, appearance is the least important of these factors. To me, the heart of executive presence is the first pillar, this idea of projecting confidence and decisiveness.

---

56   Sylvia Ann Hewlett, *Executive Presence: The Missing Link between Merit and Success* (New York: HarperCollins, 2014).

57   Hewlett, *Executive Presence.*

The feedback I get from women who are successful in leadership positions is that they have the ability to project calm certainty. Too often, in crisis situations, we can be perceived as being overly aggressive or emotional or unsteady. This perception may be biased, but it's critically important to project certainty and confidence as an executive.

I want you to understand that executive presence is real. It's very ambiguous, but people look at you, and they make a decision about whether or not you are leadership material. These three pillars are helpful ways to understand what you could be working on. Do you need to be working on your gravitas? Do you need to work on how you communicate and sell your ideas? Or do you need to be thinking about whether your appearance matches the leadership level at which you want to be operating?

These are challenging questions and require a focused awareness of your environment. What executives wear in a conservative hospital or financial setting, for example, will differ from what executives wear in a large tech company. What is executive attire in Miami will differ dramatically from executive attire in Chicago.

Branding should be a key part of your strategic effort to develop executive presence. Whether you like to think about it or not, you have a brand. It defines who you are, what you stand for, what makes you unique, special, and different, how you are great, and why you should be sought out.

A brand conveys your identity and distinctiveness. It communicates the value you offer.

If you have the wrong brand for the position you hold, or the position you want, then your work is not having the impact it could.

One of my clients came to me when she was passed over for a leadership opportunity in a large grocery store chain. She believed that she was being groomed for this role when she was made head of the cheese-buying division, a significant revenue generator for her company, and she enthusiastically embraced the role, traveling to Europe, becoming an expert on cheese, and bringing samples of new cheeses to meetings with senior leaders.

What my client didn't realize, until she sought feedback, is that she was not viewed by these executives as a potential strategic leader. She was viewed as "the cheese lady." When I spent time talking to her boss, he said that he had not thought of her for the highest levels of leadership—that was not her brand. Her brand was being "the cheese lady."

So, pause for a moment and consider your answer to these questions: What do you think your brand is? How is your brand perceived in the marketplace? Does your brand represent who you are and what you do? Or is your brand interfering with your ability to move into the C-suite?

Your answers to these questions are important, because too often your brand is all about your skills at executing rather than strategic visioning and thinking. You want to be known as a strategic resource. You want your brand to reflect your identity as someone who is insightful.

My purpose in encouraging you to examine each of these transition points is to understand that you may have outgrown your professional identity. Your brand may have supported your career goals earlier, but now it no longer reflects what you can do—or aspire to do.

Answer this question: What do you want to be known for in the next year at work—how do you want to be perceived?

As I work with students, I encourage them to step outside themselves and consider the key components of their leadership brand. Susan Hodgkinson has written extensively on this, and in her book *The Leader's Edge: Using Personal Branding to Drive Performance and*

Profit, she created the "5 Ps" to help assess how your leadership brand can be judged:[58]

- *Persona*: The emotional response others have to you as a person—the way you use your energy and style to build healthy and productive working relationships with others

- *Product* (skill): The sum of your skills, capabilities, experience, intellectual capital and potential, and results you've delivered—failures will be remembered, accomplishments soon forgotten

- *Packaging*: The visual manifestation of your leadership brand—not only your personal appearance but also your work space, your time management, your emails and voice mails

- *Promotion*: The strategic and proactive management of your reputation—making sure that the right people know about you, your team, and your work

- *Permission*: Believing that you have as much to offer, if not more, as anyone else

SORRY NOT SORRY

As you assess your leadership brand, remember that words matter; they play a role in your "packaging" by communicating confidence and authority. This is true of both spoken words (in meetings and daily interactions) and written words (in emails).

Take a moment to review this list of commonly used undermining phrases. If you recognize any as regular elements of your commu-

---

58   Susan Hodgkinson, *The Leader's Edge: Using Personal Branding to Drive Performance and Profit* (Bloomington, IN: iUniverse, 2005).

nication, understand that they may be diminishing your authority and your executive presence. Make a firm effort to eliminate them from your professional communication:

- Just: "I am just wondering …"

- Actually: "I actually disagree …"

- Kind of: "I kind of think that we should take a different approach …"

- Sorry, but: "Sorry to bother you, but …"

- A little bit: "I'd like to tell you a little bit about our new product …"

- Disclaimers: "I'm no expert, but …"

- Requests for affirmation: "Does that make sense?"

- Substituting a question for a statement: "What about increasing the marketing budget?" instead of "We need to increase the marketing budget."

- Rushing and piling on words: Interrupting your thoughts with digressions

Communication is the key to many of these arenas, and it is a critical skill for building your leadership brand. Meetings and presentations are one area where I encourage you to be attentive to how you are demonstrating this strategic leadership brand building.

In presentations, women often speak too much to process and not enough to results. Next time you're giving a presentation or watching another woman give one, see if you notice this habit. The more senior you become in an organization, the more directly you need to speak in the language of results. Your presentations should always link to corporate objectives; in fact, that should be the starting point: "Here's what I'm proposing, and this is why it links to our objectives." I advise my students and clients to start with the result and then work backward. Get to the point quickly, setting it in the context of what it means not for you but for your audience.

STRATEGIC RESOURCE

There is something quite challenging about the transition from worker bee to strategic resource because it connects in a very significant way with perception. How are you seen in the marketplace? Is your brand supporting your career goals? It's difficult to measure how effective you're being, to know whether you've accomplished the goal of ensuring that key stakeholders see you as visionary or as an executive presence.

That's why I encourage you to focus on establishing yourself as a strategic resource. What does this look like? In my world, it's how often people use me as a sounding board for ideas, new programs, new projects. How often they ask me to share insights or sit on a committee that's thinking through a new project. How often they invite me to be involved in a new initiative.

At some point, you need to separate yourself from the rest of the group. You need to be able to be known for who you are in a unique and very strategic way. You need to know—fully know— where you can add value to your organization and find confidence in that knowledge.

Reflection Points

1. Which two high-impact areas will increase your leadership influence and brand value?

\
\
\
\
\

2. What do you want to be known for in your next year of work?

\
\
\
\
\

3. Are you equating busyness with impact?

_____

_____

_____

_____

_____

PART THREE

TACTICS TO BUILD
YOUR SKILL SET

As part of your consideration of the transitions you need to make, you may have recognized that a key to this transition depends on building a certain skill. Maybe you want to move away from a place where you're berating yourself for a setback or failure and begin to view it through a lens of learning from your mistakes and building curiosity about the ways in which you are growing as a professional. Perhaps you need to practice negotiating for yourself more effectively or are wondering how to bring more of what makes you unique to your workplace in a way that is meaningful. Maybe you need to develop the muscle to overcome your fear of failure and push forward with more confidence.

In the pages that follow, you'll find four short, tip-driven chapters on the mindsets and skill sets that can help you be successful in your career. I think of these as supporting your professional comportment—the techniques to help you carry yourself for optimum growth.

CHAPTER EIGHT

NEGOTIATING FOR YOURSELF

The most common way people give up their power
is by thinking they don't have any.

–ALICE WALKER

"My boss will promote me when I'm ready."

"I'm probably getting paid what I'm worth."

"The economy is so weak that it isn't a good time to ask for more."

"There's nothing I can do to change this situation."

Do any of these statements sound familiar? If you're like most of my clients—or most women—it's likely that they do.

I called them statements, but the reality is that they are myths. In the next few pages, we'll examine precisely why we tend to believe these myths, and we'll begin to practice some active strategies to equip you to negotiate more effectively for yourself.

And the first step is by reframing how you think about this key step of asking for what you want.

I don't view this action as negotiation. Instead, I think of it as problem-solving and relationship building. I encourage you to do the same. It will shift your thinking about how to address specific issues in your workplace and in your career, not as win-lose situations but instead as ways to work toward an end of mutual benefit.

ASK FOR WHAT YOU WANT

I've been privileged to work with two women who are true experts on the challenges women face when it comes to negotiation. Linda Babcock and Sara Laschever have written extensively on this subject, including two important books that I encourage you to read: *Women Don't Ask: Negotiation and the Gender Divide* and *Ask for It: How Women Can Use the Power of Negotiation to Get What They Really Want.* Linda is the cofounder of the Carnegie Mellon Women's Executive Leadership Academy, which I now direct.

Linda's early research revealed that many women would prefer to visit the dentist for a root canal than negotiate a raise. They would rather put on a headset and listen to annoying noises, like nails on a chalkboard, than negotiate the price of a catering contract. In fact, men initiate and negotiate to advance their own interests more frequently than women do. Men negotiate more than women, especially when it comes to negotiations around compensation, benefits, titles, and other perks.[59]

What's important to note from Linda's research is this: the major gender difference in negotiation behavior is choosing to negotiate at all!

It's fascinating that, contrary to what women think, they are actually good at negotiating, and they are particularly more successful negotiating on behalf of others than for themselves. When

---

59   Linda C. Babcock, Michele Joy Gelfand, Deborah Small, and Heidi Stayn, "Gender Differences in the Propensity to Initiate Negotiations," in *Social Psychology and Economics*, eds. David De Cremer, Marcel Zeelenberg, and J. Keith Murnighan (Mahwah, NJ: Lawrence Erlbaum, 2006), 239–59.

women do choose to negotiate, they can be 14 to 23 percent more successful than men when representing others.[60] The gender gap in negotiation behavior can often be attributed to that very choice—the choice whether or not to initiate the negotiation to advance your own interests as opposed to the interests of others.

Let me add some perspective here. New research has added to our understanding of the key points highlighted in Linda's research—some suggest that women *are* asking and negotiating, but they aren't as successful as men when they do.

For example, in a 2016 study titled "Do Women Ask?," researchers were surprised to find that women actually do ask for raises as often as men—we're just more likely to be turned down.[61] Conducted by faculty at the Cass Business School, the University of Wisconsin, and the University of Warwick and using data collected from more than forty-six hundred Australian workers, the study was expected to confirm long-established theories around women's reluctance to negotiate. Instead, the analysis showed that men's and women's propensity to negotiate is roughly the same—that when comparing men and women who do similar jobs (and jobs where there are genuine opportunities for salary negotiation), women actually ask for raises at the same rates as men.

This study found that women are now negotiating as often as men—but face pushback when they do.

---

60 Hannah Riley Bowles, Linda Babcock, and Kathleen L. McGuinn, "Constraints and Triggers: Situational Mechanics of Gender in Negotiation," *Journal of Personality and Social Psychology* 89, no. 6 (2005): 951–65, https://projects.iq.harvard.edu/files/hbowles/files/situational_mechanics.pdf.

61 Benjamin Artz, Amanda H. Goodall, and Andrew J. Oswald, "Do Women Ask?," Warwick Economics Research Papers no. 1127 (July 2016), https://warwick.ac.uk/fac/soc/economics/research/workingpapers/2016/twerp_1127_oswald.pdf.

THE BROKEN RUNG

Early in this book, I talked about the obstacles we women face in our careers. We start with strong ambitions and goals and somehow, along the way, we lose the ability to advance to the top levels of leadership.

It may be helpful to think of this as a "broken rung" on the first step of the ladder to success—and the failure to advocate for ourselves contributes to this broken rung. It's this broken rung that prevents women from reaching the top. A big obstacle women face on the path to senior leadership is at the first step up to manager. For every one hundred men promoted and hired as managers, only seventy-two women are promoted and hired. This broken rung results in more women getting stuck at the entry level and fewer women becoming managers. Not surprisingly, men end up holding 62 percent of manager-level positions while women hold just 38 percent.[62]

> **A big obstacle women face on the path to senior leadership is at the first step up to manager.**

This early inequality has a long-term impact on the talent pipeline. Since men outnumber women at the manager level, there are significantly fewer women to hire or promote to senior managers. The number of women decreases at every subsequent level. So, even as hiring and promotion rates improve for women at senior levels, women as a whole can never catch up. There are simply too few women to advance.

As a result, women earn less money, progress more slowly in their careers, and don't rise as high as similarly talented men. Clearly,

---

62   McKinsey & Company and Lean In, *Women in the Workplace 2019,* accessed September 12, 2021, https://wiw-report.s3.amazonaws.com/Women_in_the_ Workplace_2019.pdf.

systems need to be built into corporate structures that focus on promoting women early on, but at the same time, women need to learn to advocate for themselves from the get go. Otherwise, the impact over a career is significant.

Let's pause here for a moment. Are you negotiating for yourself? And if not, why not?

I believe that our reluctance is connected to the ideas of agency and locus of control we discussed earlier in this book. We've been taught that relationships and following rules are important, and negotiation feels like something that could damage our relationships and break rules. That's why we don't negotiate.

Very importantly, though, we also don't negotiate because we understand intuitively that there's a backlash against women who negotiate.

There is little downside when men negotiate for themselves; people expect men to advocate on their own behalf, point out their own contributions, and be recognized and rewarded for them. For men, there truly is no harm in asking. But if women advocate for their own interests, it can easily backfire. Women are expected to be concerned with others; when they advocate for themselves or point to their own value, both men and women may react unfavorably. When a woman advocates on her own behalf, she violates perceived gender norms.

This understanding is critical. Too often, women beat themselves up for not negotiating. They criticize themselves for not being brave enough, or assertive enough, or confident enough, when really, when women negotiate for themselves, there is often a negative response. They can be considered as pushy and less likeable.

In the *Women in the Workplace 2016* study, women who negotiate reported they were 30 percent more likely than men who negotiate to receive feedback that they are "intimidating," "too aggressive," or "bossy." These are not just terms to shake off and disregard—they have an outsize impact on who wants to work with us, promote us, have us on their team, and pull us into stretch assignments. All of which have a considerable impact on our career.

We aren't stupid. We know that our attempts at negotiation can backfire.

So, what's the solution? How can we negotiate skillfully and strategically—and successfully?

HOW TO ASK

Before we talk about *what* you might negotiate for, it is just as important to be strategic about *how* you do this. How you show up for the negotiation. Your style of negotiation.

A word of warning. You're not going to like what you read here. Nobody does.

If you want to advocate for yourself, if you want to negotiate successfully as a woman, research shows that there is a right way to do it. An appropriate way to do it. A feminine way to do it.

I was right, wasn't I? You don't like this. It's upsetting and disappointing that this is the world in which we live and work.

But my point here is to equip you for successful negotiation. I said at the beginning of this book that it's important to recognize that our workplaces are gendered. If you want to successfully advocate for yourself, you'll want to use that recognition as a tool to enable you to more effectively ask for what you want.

Go ahead. Grit your teeth. But let me share some insight from Hannah Riley Bowles.[63] Professor Bowles says that there are two

---

63 Hannah Riley Bowles and Linda Babcock, "How Can Women Escape the Compensation Negotiation Dilemma? Relational Accounts Are One Answer," *Psychology of Women Quarterly* 37, no. 1 (2012), https://doi.org/10.1177/0361684312455524.

important considerations for women who are negotiating. First, you should be nice—and concerned with others. When women take a more instrumental approach—"This is what I want and deserve"—people react more negatively.

Second, you should provide a legitimate explanation for the negotiation. Men don't have to legitimize their negotiations. They are expected to look out for themselves. For women, it is different. What does this "legitimate explanation" look like? You might justify your request by saying that your team leader, for example, thought you should ask for a raise. Or you might convince your boss that your negotiating skills are good for the company—you could say, "You expect me to be a tough negotiator on your behalf with clients, so let me show you what I can do. I'll prove to you just how skilled I'll be on your behalf."

The trick then is to appear friendly, warm, and concerned for others above yourself.

Mary Sue Colman, president of the University of Michigan, describes this as being "relentlessly pleasant." Another way to describe it is "niceness with insistence."[64]

What does it look like? When you are negotiating for yourself, you want to stay composed. You want to smile. No forceful gestures—punching the air or pounding the table. This will not deliver the results you want.

So, you stay composed, and you legitimize your ask by linking it to something outside yourself.

Are you furious? I hope not. Instead, I hope that you're having a bit of an aha moment as you reflect on successful and unsuccessful negotiations you've undertaken.

---

64   Quoted in Lelia Gowland, "Why You Shouldn't Take My Advice on Women's Empowerment," *Forbes*, July 14, 2017, www.forbes.com/sites/leliagowland/2017/07/14/why-you-shouldnt-take-my-advice.

Many women, when I share this information, will ask legitimate questions. Things like "Aren't we just keeping the same power structure in place?"

Yes, possibly. But I want to be pragmatic in this book. I want to share strategies that you can use today, not in some hopefully not too distant future when workplaces are different. My goal is for you to be in the "room where it happens" to gain the access you can then use to create change from within. Once you are in the room, you can change the rules. So perhaps, if you normally come into a negotiation more forcefully, you might want to try a different approach to see if it's more effective.

WHAT TO ASK FOR

Everything.

Too often, we compartmentalize before we even ask, talking ourselves out of specific requests because we believe "they'll never agree to that."

I encourage you to begin from a place of relentless pleasantness, with the idea that everything is negotiable. Yes, *everything*.

Starting date. Signing bonus. Office location. Office size. Work hours. Pregnancy leave. Moving expenses. Sabbaticals. Tuition assistance. Retirement contributions.

All of these are negotiable. And negotiations can happen at any time, not just annually around performance reviews. So often when we think about negotiation, we tend to think immediately and solely about compensation but fail to think more broadly about how the opportunity at hand fits into our long-term career goals and how we could also be negotiating for items that support our career advancement—things like scope of authority, resources for the role, and development opportunities that could benefit your long-term career more than how simply negotiating your pay and benefits does in the short term. Both are important, and you should not be afraid to ask for both.

It helps to enter any negotiation with a best alternative in mind—your plan B (or in negotiation speak, your BATNA: best alternative to a negotiated agreement). This is your biggest source of power in a negotiation. Think for a moment: If you don't get what you want, what will you do? What is your fallback position? It might be to maintain the status quo; it might be something else.

If you identify your best alternative, you have options. You can walk away. And that's a very powerful position to be in.

You also want to know your bottom line. What is the point beyond which you won't go?

And finally, you want to know the outcome you're hoping for. What is the best outcome for this negotiation?

I encourage clients to use what we call, in the Carnegie Mellon Women's Executive Leadership Academy, the "giggle test." If you can name your price, your title, your ask, without giggling, it's a legitimate ask.

Identifying your own BATNA, reservation price, and target price is not enough. You must also try to identify your counterpart's BATNA, reservation price, and target price.

DO YOUR HOMEWORK

The biggest difference between a successful and an unsuccessful negotiation will be your preparation. Part of this planning should be thinking about the other negotiator; specifically, you should spend time thinking about and actively planning for

> **The biggest difference between a successful and an unsuccessful negotiation will be your preparation.**

what the other person will want and what will be helpful to them. Learn what's negotiable, how you can negotiate for what you want—and with whom.

Don't negotiate by discussing how good you are at your job. Don't discuss your aptitude. Instead, focus on your *impact*. What specifically can you do to save your organization money or earn money for your organization?

Get out of your own head and get into the head of the other person. Think about what matters to them, what's important to them.

I said it at the beginning of this chapter. If the thought of "negotiating" is troublesome, reframe what you are doing. Instead, think of it as problem-solving or relationship building. Speak of your—and their—"interests" or "concerns" rather than framing it as a "position." Perhaps there doesn't need to be one "winner"—instead, you can identify how to ensure that both of you trade "wins" in a way that is advantageous to you and your negotiating counterpart.

What are you afraid of? Is it that you will hear the word *no*? No is simply a starting point for the negotiation; it's not the end point of the negotiation. Get comfortable with that first no. When you hear it, say to yourself, "Yes!" Yes—the negotiation is underway. Yes—I am going to practice the skills and strategies I've prepared. Yes—I am solving a problem that I need to resolve.

I'm sure that you've heard, many times, that you won't get what you want unless you ask for it. Instead, I prefer to see it this way: It's important to keep asking. Essential, even. The more we do it, the more opportunities we give employers to say yes, to notice pay discrepancies among their workers, and to grapple with their own biases.

Reflection Points

1. Which small, low-stake issue can you practice negotiating for—something that you'd like but don't really care if you get, something that is easy for the other person to give you?

   _____

   _____

   _____

   _____

   _____

2. What are four to five things you'd like to negotiate (include at least one no-brainer and one big "ask" on your list)? What do you want (positions), and why do you want it (interests)? Equally, what does your counterpart want, and why do they want it?

   _____

   _____

   _____

   _____

   _____

3. Which strategic choices do you need to make, and what preparation will you need to equip you to negotiate for all of these things?

_____

_____

_____

_____

_____

CHAPTER NINE

CONFIDENT IS NOT HOW YOU FEEL

I've been absolutely terrified every moment of my life—and I've never let it keep me from doing a single thing I wanted to do.

—GEORGIA O'KEEFFE

I regularly coach clients and students on leadership skills, and confidence is a key element in projecting a leadership presence. Because of the work I do, and the way I present myself, people assume that I am a confident person.

So, let me share a little insight, inspired by Georgia O'Keeffe: I am often afraid.

As I think about confidence, I'm reminded of my arrival with my family in the United States about twenty years ago. We had flown into the Pittsburgh airport in February—not a good month to move to Pittsburgh. I was an experienced traveler by this point, adept at moving and starting over in a new place, but there was something about how miserably bleak Pittsburgh looked in that wintry weather. I may have been travel weary, I may have been tired of moving, but I simply froze in fear. I was suddenly unwilling to learn to drive on the right-hand side of the road, to battle the cold and the snow. I refused to leave the airport and start my new life in Pittsburgh.

Imagine the scene if you can: my husband, my two young sons, and me, camped out in an Au Bon Pain café near the security checkpoint, surrounded by our luggage and belongings, while I try to muster the necessary courage to leave the airport.

Of course, eventually I was ready. But it took a long time. And I would love to tell you that that was my last major lapse in courage, but of course it wasn't.

For a long time, I really wanted to get to a place where I would feel consistently brave and fearless, but what I have come to learn is that I—and the many women I coach—can be highly successful, even if we are terrified. You can be afraid and do things anyway. You do not have to be fearless. It's okay to be terrified, but to achieve anything of value in your life or your career, you have to just do it, regardless of how frightened you may be.

Confidence is not a feeling. It's an action.

You are never going to feel entirely confident, and you may waste time trying to get to that point. Instead, my goal for you in this chapter is to encourage you to learn to live with the discomfort of not feeling very confident at any point. Because the biggest problem is that when you do not feel confident, you may be tempted to hesitate at critical times in your career, and that's what comes back to hurt you.

THE CONFIDENCE CONTINUUM

Earlier in this book, I discussed an exercise I do in the classroom around gender, where I ask students to position themselves in a line based on how they self-identify. I do a similar exercise around confidence.

Take a moment now to imagine where you would position yourself if you were in my classroom. Picture that one wall represents 100 percent confidence and the other 0 percent confidence. How confident are you? Where would you stand if you were participating in this exercise—close to the highly confident end point, near the weak end point, or somewhere in the middle? Would where you stand be different if you were thinking about your personal life versus your professional life?

As we've discussed earlier, confidence and aspiration erode for women at the midpoint in their careers in a way that doesn't happen for their male peers. And it's important to build the skill of keeping yourself confident in what you bring to the table. Consider for a moment the situations and circumstances in which you've experienced the most self-doubt. For many women—perhaps for you—self-doubt is triggered by moments when you're questioning your competence, your ability to manage and succeed in a specific situation.

When you choose not to act, when you hesitate because you aren't sure, you hold yourself back at key moments in your career. It might be applying for a new job or volunteering for a presentation. You may shy away from a promotion and self-select out of new opportunities because you think you are underqualified. This hesitation has consequences.

I want to dig deeper here and unpack exactly why this is relevant. Confidence is a belief in your ability to succeed, a belief that stimulates action. In turn, taking action bolsters your belief in your ability to succeed. Recognize the paradox here: confidence accumulates—through hard work, through success, and even through failure.

Confidence can transform your thoughts into judgments about what you can do. Confidence then transforms those judgments into action. So, confidence is the fuel that you can harness to turn your thoughts into actions.

> **Confidence is the fuel that you can harness to turn your thoughts into actions.**

Action should be the focus here, because confidence is linked to doing. In fact, one of the essential ingredients in confidence is action—the belief that you can succeed at things and make them happen.

This requires a conscious decision on your part to not allow your doubts to consume you. You have to take those steps away from your comfort zone to try something new and do hard things. Yes, *do* hard things instead of just thinking about doing them.

It's important to recognize that you will never get to a point in your life or your career when you will magically feel able to cope with all situations. If you are truly pushing yourself, and challenging yourself, and trying new things, you will not feel completely confident.

So how do you learn to manage this? How do you deal with being in new situations, not feeling confident, but taking action in spite of it?

LOSE AND MOVE FORWARD

My sons have learned many lessons from participating in competitive sports, but one of the most significant is their ability to lose and move on.

They don't ruminate. They aren't devastated by the loss. They don't spend endless hours worrying that they are no good. They accept the loss and keep going.

What fascinates me about this is that, too often, I see women attribute failures internally—"I'm no good. Why did I even try this?

I'll never do this again"—when external factors may have been responsible for a failure.

We address this at the university by encouraging students to fail forward fast. The goal is to make a mistake so that you can learn, so that you can do better next time.

If you study entrepreneurs, what makes them successful is this ability to fail forward fast. It's not necessarily their ideas, their backing, or the funds to which they have access. It's how quickly they can launch a product, fail, try again, fail, launch, sell, try again. It's the speed with which they fail, learn from that failure, and move on.

How can you begin to develop this ability? The first step is to avoid overthinking. It may sound challenging to consciously not overthink, but women are much more likely than men to ruminate, and excessive examination actually inhibits confidence because it can keep you from taking action.

Consider this: You're debating whether to recommend a course of action at work. It's a tough call, and you dig in to examine both sides in-depth. But your examination takes so long that you start to lose your ability to make a decision. You feel frozen and decide not to weigh in.

In today's business climate, failing means you've been willing to try, to get in the game. And it means you've learned.

CONFIDENCE TRUMPS COMPETENCE

Too many women hesitate, deciding to wait until they feel competent enough for an opportunity, a challenge, a job, a promotion. They incorrectly assume that confidence will come once they feel competent.

My encouragement to you is to rethink this ordering of priorities. If you are willing to fail—if, in fact, you can accept it as a necessary step—you will feel more confident, which will lead you toward building the very competence you think you need.

I love what conductor Benjamin Zander says about leadership and problem-solving. He stresses the importance of facing problems not with resignation or anger but with a sense of possibility. By choosing possibility, and challenging assumptions (even our own), he says, we move toward excellence.

In his graduate class at the New England Conservatory, Zander gives each of his students an A at the beginning of the year. This is a highly competitive program, and the students, when they arrive, are focused on being the best. Zander counters this by immediately awarding them all an A and then asks them to write a letter describing who they will have become by the following May when the class ends. Teachers (and society at large), he notes, tend to treat A students quite differently from students who are given a C-minus.

When asked to explain the effect of this practice, Zander replies:[65]

"When students are given an unconditional 'A' in the first class of the year, and describe in a letter dated in the future who they have become over the year, it makes the students and the teacher committed partners on a fascinating and joyful journey, where, for the time being, standards are in the background, and there is no striving—just engagement, participation, and expression. They are liberated from fear to do the work they have always wanted to do, and their performance, we have discovered, is likely to surprise and delight their teachers, themselves, and all who hear them."

When Zander's musicians make a mistake, he teaches them not to give in to the voice of doubt or self-recrimination. Instead, he has

---

65   Rosamund Stone Zander and Benjamin Zander, *The Art of Possibility* (New York: Penguin, 2006).

instructed his students to say "How fascinating!" whenever they make a mistake. To Zander, this means throwing up one's arms and exclaiming "How fascinating!" at top volume. His point: Every setback is an opportunity to learn. Every setback represents a world of possibility.

CONFIDENCE CAVEATS

I encourage the women I work with not to confuse doubt about the work they've done with self-doubt. If you're questioning the work, that's good! That's what a leader does. It's important to ask strategic questions like: Are we heading in the right direction? Are we doing the right thing?

Asking these questions doesn't imply a lack of confidence. It reflects thoughtful leadership. Being a thoughtful leader means that you are consistently questioning whether or not there's a better way, a different market, a more efficient process.

That's my first confidence caveat. The second is this: Know the rules. You've probably heard the following statistic: Men apply for a job when they meet only 60 percent of the qualifications, but women apply only if they meet 100 percent of them.

The finding comes from a Hewlett-Packard internal report, and it has been quoted in books like *Lean In* and *The Confidence Code*, and it's been included in dozens of articles. It's usually invoked as evidence that women need more confidence.

But I respectfully disagree. What's needed isn't more confidence—it's a clearer understanding of what those qualifications actually mean. The women who weren't applying believed they needed the qualifications not to do the job well but to be hired in the first place. They thought that the required qualifications were … well, *required* qualifications. They didn't see the hiring process as one where advocacy, relationships, or a creative approach to framing one's expertise could overcome not having the skills and experiences outlined in the job qualifications.

What held them back from applying was not a mistaken perception about themselves but a mistaken perception about the hiring process.

This is critical because it suggests that if the hiring process finding speaks to a larger trend, women don't need to try to find that elusive quality—"confidence." They simply need better information about how hiring processes really work.

The women I work with tend to be very confident in their skills, so I don't see lack of confidence as the problem here. Instead, I think it's a lack of understanding of what the rules are. They need more information about the true rules governing any specific situation to understand which rules can be broken and when.

This brings us to my third caveat: the problem with unconscious bias. Women are often penalized for a perceived lack of confidence and also for displays of confidence. It's a vicious circle—women who aren't perceived as confident are not deemed to have executive presence, but when they behave assertively, they are perceived as overly aggressive. It's a delicate balance, this idea that confidence must be placed within a social context and with an awareness of how your actions and behavior are being perceived by others.

I want to note here that the data show us that Black women, lesbian and bisexual women, and women with disabilities have their competence and judgment questioned more often than White women (and certainly men).[66] A discussion of confidence—and of the earlier perspective of making mistakes and learning from them—is complicated, as these women will be viewed through a different lens and are more likely to be "penalized" for errors. These confidence caveats

---

66   McKinsey & Company and Lean In, *Women in the Workplace 2019.*

are particularly important. It's critical to understand the rules. Your approach to avoiding hesitation, taking action, and making mistakes may need to be slightly more calculated as a result.

It's helpful to consider this through the lens of what is known in social psychology as the "stereotype content model." This is a model that suggests that we use two dimensions to judge others: competence and warmth. The research on unconscious bias and women around confidence shows us that men are seen as confident if they are viewed as competent, but women are viewed as confident only if they come across as both competent *and warm*.[67] As a result, women must be seen as warm in order to capitalize on their competence—and to be viewed as confident—while competent men are seen as confident whether or not they are viewed as warm.

Consider the research we discussed earlier about the double bind. We tend to put women in this trade-off situation where they are either seen as liked (or, in this case, warm) but not competent or seen as competent but not liked.

So, the challenge for all of us is to determine how best to maintain—or increase—our relational warm skills while at the same time communicating our competence. One strategy I encourage you to consider is to review your communication skills (you'll find helpful tips in chapter 7). If you want to project both warmth and competence, at a minimum you'll want to be sure to not use disempowering language. A small act (or word selection) can make an outsize difference. And if confident isn't necessarily what you feel in a given situation, think about how you can project a sense of confidence to others.

---

67   Margarita Mayo, "To Seem Confident, Women Have to Be Seen as Warm," *Harvard Business Review*, July 8, 2016, https://hbr.org/2016/07/to-seem-confident-women-have-to-be-seen-as-warm.

If you are naturally warm and have been concerned that perceptions of your competence will take a knock because you are seen as "likable," you can be encouraged in this research that, to seem confident, women have to been seen as warm. However, a word of warning: you, too, will need to avoid the trap of using disempowering language.

I realize that your head is likely spinning trying to make sense of all of this, and you're probably frustrated at how unfair this seems. It is frustrating, and hard, but it's important for us as women to see and understand the evidence for what it takes for women to succeed in a biased world.

ENTER THE BRAVE ZONE

There's been a lot of discussion in the university world of creating "safe zones" for students. Safe zones are important and incredibly vital when it comes to building confidence and being with people with similar experiences. In my classes, I also like to encourage students to choose to move into a "brave zone"—a space where you will be not only challenged but also where you can really stretch yourself in a conscious way. The only way in which you will grow and be successful is at the very edges of your comfort zone.

> **The only way in which you will grow and be successful is at the very edges of your comfort zone.**

Recognize that this means that if you are constantly growing and changing and doing new things, you will never feel 100 percent confident.

I sensed, as I prepared to write this chapter, that many of you would turn here first, looking for a magic formula for confidence. There's a belief among many women that not feeling confident is a problem that they want to solve. We want to learn confidence, study confidence, master confidence.

But I hope that this chapter has encouraged you to think differently, to understand that a rich life, full of challenges and new opportunities and growth, will require you to feel a little uncomfortable, a little lacking in confidence.

Whenever I am terrified to do something—like leaving that airport twenty years ago—I ask myself one question: "Does this help me become the person I imagine myself becoming?"

If the answer is yes—if growing into the person I want to be requires me to do this very thing that scares me—then regardless of how terrified I am, I do it.

Don't be afraid of trying or failing. Embrace the opportunity to call out "How fascinating!" and to experience all of the possibilities that lie just outside your comfort zone.

Reflection Points

1. What strategies do you need to practice to avoid ruminating and overthinking?

_____

_____

_____

_____

_____

2. When do you experience the most self-doubt—and why?

_____

_____

_____

_____

_____

3. What is holding you back from becoming the person you want to be?

_____

_____

_____

_____

_____

CHAPTER TEN

DON'T BERATE YOURSELF; BE CURIOUS

*Everything you're sure is right can
be wrong in another place.*

—BARBARA KINGSOLVER

A t different stages of your career, you need different things—different skills, different tactics. You will show up in your career in a different way, and what's important will change.

The preceding chapters have shown that you won't make progress by standing on the sidelines. Yet, you hesitate. You do not seize the leadership opportunities available to you. You listen to your inner critic.

And this is understandable, because if you step off the sidelines, you will make mistakes. You will fail. And research shows us that women are judged more harshly for their mistakes than men and may respond by being more risk averse, a tendency often exacerbated by the quest for perfection.[68] As we've discussed earlier, this "perfect or bust" thinking can get us into trouble.

Just think about where we normally experience this all-or-nothing thinking. For many of us, it's a mindset around fitness or dieting goals, where we seem to operate only in extremes. We move from a deep commitment to an exercise routine to despair and sitting on the couch eating cookie dough.

Now, consider this from a career perspective. Consider the implications if the only option is complete perfection. If you experience a setback or a failure, you may plummet into despair and wallow in questioning who you are to even think you could succeed at this (fill in the blank with a task/job/challenge).

But if you aspire to leadership, you must be prepared to fail. As you rise in your career, the roles become less specifically defined, less structured, and riskier. Leaders cannot adopt all-or-nothing thinking. They don't see their missteps as the end of the world or the end of their career but as an opportunity to think through problems creatively and figure out how to be stronger leaders.

This kind of resilience—the ability to bounce back and move forward (the speed and strength of your response to adversity)—is more available to people who are curious about their own way of thinking and behaving.

THE CURIOSITY ANTIDOTE

If you wrestle with perfectionism and all-or-nothing thinking, I have an antidote: curiosity. Instead of giving in to the temptation to beat

---

68   Catherine H. Tinsley and Robin J. Ely, "What Most People Get Wrong about Men and Women," *Harvard Business Review*, May-June 2018, https://hbr.org/2018/05/what-most-people-get-wrong-about-men-and-women?autocomplete=true.

yourself up, to say, "I failed—I'm terrible at this," be curious. Ask yourself probing questions such as "Why did I do this?" and "How did I do this?" and "What have I learned from this?" and "How do I move forward?" and maybe "What could I do differently next time?"

If you aspire to leadership, you need to be curious about all things—including yourself. The question is not whether or not you will fail but how you will recover.

> **If you aspire to leadership, you need to be curious about all things— including yourself.**

Curiosity about yourself—your thinking and behavior—is a vital tool, one that you should begin to use today. There will be many areas of your personal and professional life in which you don't have agency; you do have control over how you treat yourself. Be a good friend to yourself. Why make yourself feel worse when you can make yourself feel better?

If you're feeling weighed down by stress or setbacks, if you're struggling with this idea of what it looks like to be curious about yourself, I have a challenge for you. Come up with an alter ego for yourself, the best version of your fiercest self. Give your alter ego a name, go to your local coffee shop, and order a beverage in her name. When you hear that name called, play the game of being curious about this person. Who is she? Why did she order this specific drink on this specific day? How has her day unfolded so far? What is she going to accomplish in the next twenty-four hours?

It may sound silly, but there are opportunities to have fun around the idea of curiosity. Curiosity shouldn't be a heavy burden; instead, it should be an inviting reminder to think in new ways about yourself and the world around you.

Curiosity can be defined as a penchant for seeking new experiences, knowledge, and feedback and for demonstrating an openness to change. And it is a key skill if you are aspiring to leadership.

All-or-nothing thinking is dysfunctional. It's the opposite of curious. And it's closely associated with increased risks of depression, anxiety, and hopelessness. Learning to be more curious is vital, not only for your professional life but also for a healthy personal life.

Think about how you look at the world. Do you have hope? Are you optimistic and interested to discover what's next? Are you grateful for the many things in front of you that provide opportunities to learn and grow?

STRATEGICALLY CURIOUS

The good news is that curiosity is not genetic. It can be learned, encouraged, and developed in everyone.

Curiosity is good for you. When your curiosity is triggered, you'll think more deeply and rationally about decisions and come up with more creative solutions.

> **Curiosity is a key marker for innovative thinking.**

And there are clear, business-centric reasons to develop this skill. Curiosity is a key marker for innovative thinking. Recruiters consistently mention wanting candidates who are curious. The ability to demonstrate curiosity through small talk and social interactions is yet another critical skill for leaders. We discussed earlier the importance of building networks of influence; this skill supports a strategy based on relationship building rather than on transactional agreements.

So, what can you do to avoid self-criticism and instead adopt a mindset of curiosity? Here are some strategies to consider.

Getting to Know You

Too often in the business world, social interactions can become purely transactional. One way around this is to challenge yourself to learn three facts about a peer or colleague. Frame it in the form of curiosity: "I'm curious to learn why this person _____." Perhaps you'd like to learn about why a colleague joined your organization, or something about their hometown, or you are interested in a book that they're reading. It doesn't have to be work-centered. The point is to demonstrate and practice curiosity by learning about others.

Frame Your Failures

I've spoken before about the importance of failing forward fast, identifying mistakes and setbacks as opportunities for learning and growth. This is an important strategy for curiosity—recognizing how to frame these setbacks and opportunities. My goal here is for you to reflect upon a situation that might feel like a failure and instead of ruminating or engaging in self-criticism, note down what you've learned and how you've grown from this experience.

Try this tactic: Each day, make a note of one mistake you've made, what you've learned, and what you will do differently next time. Recognize that you'll make mistakes—daily—but each will present an opportunity for curiosity and growth. Then note one good thing that happened on that day.

Interrupt the Story

Sometimes we tell ourselves stories that simply aren't true. We notice that a team member is distracted in a meeting and assume that it's because they hated our presentation. A client chooses not to sign a contract and we assume it's because we didn't do an effective job pitching the opportunity. If you find yourself spiraling into crazy conclusions, interrupt the story. Be curious about the truth. Go to the person involved and ask. Check the facts.

There's also value in examining your history. If you've successfully led a meeting or pitched a service in the past, you can begin to consider why this particular opportunity had a different outcome. What is different? What's changed?

You may choose to ask whether it even matters. The "rule of seven" is quite helpful to me—will this matter in seven days? Seven weeks? Seven years?

Finally, you can get out of your head by getting into your body. Exercise, a brisk walk, or yoga are all amazing strategies to use to interrupt the story if you're tempted to ruminate.

Build Your Circle

Curiosity is contagious. Choose who you spend time with. Engage with people who are different—who will open your mind to new experiences and support your efforts to learn new things. When you surround yourself with people who are curious about others and about the world, their curiosity will be infectious.

ASKING THE RIGHT QUESTIONS

I've found meditation to be a powerful tool when I am battling self-criticism. Curiosity depends on asking good questions, thoughtful questions, questions directed toward learning and growth.

My workplace meditation may be helpful to you as you begin to make a shift from critique to curiosity:

The One Tool

The one thing to do right now is to go and be quiet. Yes, go and sit somewhere with no distraction. No pinging texts, no incoming mail, no Skype, no Zoom, no Microsoft Teams. No background TV or radio, no kids, no distraction. Let's try this for just five minutes.

Now, simply breathe in and breathe out. As you breathe in, breathe in all your frustration or anger or sadness, and when you breathe out, breathe out spaciousness and relief. It may help to close your eyes while you do this.

When you feel you are sitting more comfortably and some of the tightness has left your body, ask, "What am I longing for?" and listen to whatever comes up. There may be a long list. That's fine. Just keep listening and asking, "What else?"

When you have expressed to yourself what you long for, ask the question, "Why? To what purpose do I want these things?"

When you have reflected on your reasons for wanting what you do, ask, "When I get up from this place, what do I want to do differently? How do I make it real?" Be specific by asking what you need to commit to do straightaway.

Before leaving your quiet spot, and still with your eyes closed, shift from wanting it to having it, and then send a thought or a wish to an individual you know, or a group, or everyone who you think is in a similar situation.

This is for on-the-spot crises kind of relief. It can be done anywhere, at any time—before a sales pitch, before you resign, after a fight, after a long day while you are sitting in your car in your garage summoning the energy for the evening shift of suppertime, bath time, bedtime.

The point is to create a pause in your full catastrophe kind of living.

I want you to aim for a small moment, an opportunity to redirect how the next moments of your life play out. Each time that you pause and ask these questions, you can begin to move in a direction of your conscious and intentional choosing, guided by your curiosity.

Reflection Points

1. What three steps will you take today to demonstrate curiosity?

   _____

   _____

   _____

   _____

   _____

2. When you experience a setback today—or tomorrow— which specific questions will you ask yourself to ensure that you continue to push forward?

   _____

   _____

   _____

   _____

   _____

3. Who do you know who consistently demonstrates curiosity and engagement with their world and with other people?

_____

_____

_____

_____

_____

CHAPTER ELEVEN

THE QUEST FOR AUTHENTICITY

(Hint: It's Overrated)

Unless you're Oprah, "Be yourself"
is terrible advice.

—ADAM GRANT

I have never taught in any women's leadership programming where the quest for authenticity did not come up as a topic for discussion. There are a myriad of reasons for the ubiquitous appearance of this topic, which we will unpack in this chapter; however, to frame the conversations in these programs, I often share with participants Adam Grant's article, the title of which is the opening quote for this chapter: "Unless you're Oprah, 'Be yourself' is terrible advice."[69]

---

69   Adam Grant, "Unless You're Oprah, 'Be Yourself' Is Terrible Advice," *New York Times*, June 4, 2016, www.nytimes.com/2016/06/05/opinion/sunday/unless-youre-oprah-be-yourself-is-terrible-advice.html.

There are always a variety of responses to Grant's article, some quite visceral. The following are just a sample:

> *I am repelled by the assertion that being my authentic self is a terrible idea. I don't subscribe to the notion that my authentic self is a raw, impulsive, unaware, "truth-hurts" shadow self. My authentic self is the best self that I aspire to be and am. My current best authentic self is growing and improving daily through awareness, practice, and pursuit of alignment between my strengths, goals, motivators, and opportunities.*

And on the other side of the continuum:

> *I loved this article—the idea of bringing the outside in, rather than leading with one's raw self, emotions and all, really resonated with me. I'm not a person that shares personal information easily and the concept of "authenticity," while laudable for many, has always felt too personal for my comfort.*

I suspect that you had a response when you read this chapter's opening quote, even without having read the article. If you were sitting with us, you would see how the conversation would go to definitions. What do we mean by authenticity and disclosure? How much vulnerability at work is too much? Are authenticity and professionalism diametrically opposed to one another?

We would touch on comfort zones and growth mindsets, on timing and stage in career, on power and status and who has it and who does not and what this means for the notion of being true to ourselves.

It's always a nuanced, thoughtful conversation, with people settling on their own opinion based on their stage in career, the level of their role, the context they operate in, and their aspirations.

My worry is that as concepts such as "authenticity" and "vulnerability" have become more mainstream in leadership conversations, there is an error to either oversimplify or conflate these concepts in ways that hurt a woman's career. In terms of oversimplification, many equate full disclosure with vulnerability. Even Brené Brown is very clear that "vulnerability minus boundaries is not vulnerability."[70]

There is now a management style known as "vulnerable leadership," in which being vulnerable is not an act or a behavior but is rather framed as a management tool. The idea is that there is strength and courage in being vulnerable—in being open in our professional lives, in removing the protective armor and revealing our true selves. Specifically, it was described as a "soft skills superpower" for women, implying that women are better equipped to lead with vulnerability.[71]

I don't find this concept very helpful. My belief is that empathy—not vulnerability—is the critical superpower for leaders, regardless of gender. One of the most important lessons in leadership is that ultimately, it's not about *you*. It's about those who are following you, those who are looking to you for leadership. It's about who they are, what they need, and where you are leading them. Your goal as a leader should be to focus on what will help your team move in a specific direction in service of the common goals you have. While vulnerability is important in a leader, its application needs to be thoughtful and intentional. Leaders must avoid the temptation to be hyperfocused on themselves and instead should be focused on the needs of those around them.

Empathy—*not* sympathy, which is about feelings of sorrow and pity for someone else's misfortune versus the ability to be aware of, under-

---

70 Jessica Stillman, "How Much Vulnerability at Work Is Too Much? Brené Brown Just Explained in 6 Words," *Inc.*, March 5, 2021, www.inc.com/jessica-stillman/brene-brown-leadership-vulnerability-authenticity.html.

71 Diana McKeon Charkalis, "The Line between Vulnerability and Oversharing," Forge, July 3, 2020, https://forge.medium.com/the-line-between-vulnerability-and-oversharing-74377e68ccd5.

stand, and appreciate the feelings and thoughts of others, an important distinction—supports this focus. Where vulnerability requires a focus on oneself, empathy is about putting yourself in the shoes of the other. If sharing more of yourself will support that goal, it's fine—but identify clearly what your team needs and work to help them.

What does this look like? When we hold our weekly team meetings, we start with a quick check-in, a way to find out the answer to the question, "Where is everybody at?" (to use a Pittsburgh expression). As a leader, it would be disingenuous if, during these conversations, I was always upbeat. At the same time, during challenging moments, my team wants me to demonstrate strong leadership, to inspire them with the confidence that I have our goals and our mission in sight—to convey determination, purpose, and a sense of forward motion.

I understand the need for a true response to demonstrate connection and our common humanity. But leaders must inspire confidence, and that confidence can be disrupted if we are too vulnerable, if we reveal each moment when we feel overwhelmed, concerned, or unsettled. Your team needs vision and guidance. If you aspire to be a leader, your priority must be on how to equip your team to achieve its goals.

> **If you aspire to be a leader, your priority must be on how to equip your team to achieve its goals.**

I appreciate this quote from Jessica Stillman: "Our loved ones are there to help us bear our emotional burdens. Our colleagues are there to help us accomplish great things together."[72] I find this a very helpful lens through which to think about what to professionally share.

Jeffrey Pfeffer, a professor of organizational behavior at Stanford's Graduate School of Business, has written extensively on leadership

---

72   Stillman, "How Much Vulnerability at Work Is Too Much?"

and how effective leaders impact their organizations. He says, "One of the most important leadership skills is the ability to put on a show, to act like a leader, to act in a way that inspires confidence and garners support—even if the person doing the performance does not actually feel confident or powerful."[73]

There's something quite significant in this perspective. I've discussed, earlier in this book, the importance of reflecting on what inspires real passion and purpose in you. But as a leader, you must take that awareness and knowledge with you and harness them to achieve very specific and clear goals. There are times when your team, your role, your mission, will require you to, in Pfeffer's words, "act like a leader," even if that is inauthentic.

That's why I say in this chapter's title that authenticity is overrated.

YOUR "TRUE" SELF

So many of the women I work with share their frustration at the feedback they're receiving. Too often it's not helpful—there's a constant theme of either not being enough or being too much of something. It's exhausting to constantly try to navigate between being too soft and too hard, being ambitious but "ladylike," without ever achieving that elusive sense of being exactly right. There's a sense that leadership requires you to "act like a man," and yet, when you do so, too often you are criticized for being too aloof, too judgmental, too harsh.

It's not surprising that, in this climate, a philosophy that advocates for authenticity and vulnerability would be attractive. So many women simply want to show up as they are in the workplace.

---

73   Jeffrey Pfeffer, *Leadership BS: Fixing Workplaces and Careers One Truth at a Time* (New York: HarperCollins, 2015), 98.

But we need to be careful about simply adopting another leadership strategy because it's become fashionable. Step back and consider what you want in your leaders. Do you want someone who openly shares every fear and doubt? A leader who is true to themselves by expressing their inner thoughts and feelings and not masking what's going on in their heads? Or a leader who discloses enough of their emotions and experiences to move the work, the team's connection, and your relationship with them forward? Personally, I so appreciate a leader who shares enough of who they are to build trust and connection but not so much that I feel overwhelmed, depleted, or immobilized by their emotions and worries. I am grateful for any leader who sets a constructive tone, allowing us to move forward with confidence, as opposed to getting mired in the quicksand of all the natural fears and worries and anxieties that make up organizational life and living.

I understand the allure of vulnerable leadership. It can be inviting to picture yourself in a meeting, unburdening yourself to your team members, sharing your questions, your fatigue. At the end of a session like that, you will feel better. And there certainly is a way to share true concerns—to be human. This is how we build trust and connection. However, the trick is not to discredit yourself, undermine your career, or create debilitating angst in the places you work.

The problem is that it can backfire for women. You lose credibility and effectiveness as a leader if you disclose everything you think and feel, especially when you are unproven. First impressions form quickly, and they matter. Expressing vulnerability too early on can make people question your ability to do the job, judging you as weak or unprofessional. As Adam Grant says, "When we broadcast our limitations, we need to be careful to avoid casting doubt on our strengths."

It's vital to understand this nuance, walking the line between authenticity and professionalism. You must demonstrate competence first; you have to have status. It's important to know that your team—your organization—will always want a leader with a certain level of confidence in charge.

Many times, the women I coach will say, "That's just not me," when I share a strategy or encourage them to try one of the tactics we've discussed in this book.

Perhaps you've shared this sentiment as you've moved through the chapters and considered the techniques I've recommended.

That's just not me.

This is perhaps one of the biggest internal obstacles women face on their leadership journey, this sense that negotiating more strategically or approaching setbacks from a position of curiosity or presenting an attitude of confidence and optimism is inauthentic and therefore not valuable. How can you develop and grow as a leader, as a professional, if your default response to new opportunities and new postures is "That's just not me"?

You've picked up this book because you're trying to get somewhere else. The way to do that is to select a new direction and try different behaviors, and of course they're not going to feel like "you" initially.

My worry is that authenticity can become a barrier, something to hide behind. It's critical to recognize that the behaviors and attitudes that have led you to a certain point in your career can then become obstacles. The saying "What got you here won't get you there" has real resonance. Let me encourage you to be willing to try new behaviors and to stretch yourself.

I reject the belief that we have one "true" self. I've quoted Herminia Ibarra elsewhere in this book, but her writing on this topic is extremely thoughtful. She says:[74]

---

74 Herminia Ibarra, "The Authenticity Paradox," *Harvard Business Review*, January-February 2015, https://hbr.org/2015/01/the-authenticity-paradox.

Career advances require all of us to move way beyond our comfort zones. At the same time, however, they trigger a strong countervailing impulse to protect our identities: When we are unsure of ourselves or our ability to perform well or measure up in a new setting, we often retreat to familiar behaviors and styles. But my research also demonstrates that the moments that most challenge our sense of self are the ones that can teach us the most about leading effectively. By viewing ourselves as works in progress and evolving our professional identities through trial and error, we can develop a personal style that feels right to us and suits our organizations' changing needs.

In reality, we have multiple selves. We aspire to different things, which may be quite different from where we are today. Those aspirations often require us to grow and change. And when we focus too much on questions of authenticity, we linger in the belief that there is only one true self—one true version of who we are or can be.

A colleague of mine, Michelle Stoner, expresses this in a lovely and powerful way that I'm thinking about as I write this chapter. Michelle is consistently raising the bar when it comes to critical thinking and sensemaking in service to self-awareness. In a variety of business meetings and settings, she quotes the Walt Whitman poem "Song of Myself, 51": "Do I contradict myself? Very well then I contradict myself. (I am large, I contain multitudes.)"

SHIFT YOUR FOCUS

This is why I stressed at the beginning of this chapter the idea of empathy as an alternative to authenticity. Leaders need to be externally focused, deeply aware of their environment and the key stakeholders in it.

Empathy is a much more helpful way to consider this as a skill to support your leadership goals. It requires you to be aware of who you are but in the context of others. Empathy will equip you to understand your team better—to know what motivates them, what matters to them, and what they'll need to move purposefully toward key organizational goals.

> Leaders need to be externally focused, deeply aware of their environment and the key stakeholders in it.

That's a leadership skill set. That's a true superpower.

My message is not to shift like a chameleon, shedding selves and identities in response to every new group or situation. No, what I'm recommending is that you adopt the posture of a situational leader, choosing to be effective in response to what your team needs and what your organization requires.

The encouragement to "just be yourself" is so pervasive, but pause for a moment and consider. Is it enough to be yourself? Or do you want to be better? What does it mean to be yourself, and is that what you want to bring into the workplace at all times and in all ways?

Feeling like a fake—even an imposter—can be a sign of growth. It may mean that you're trying something new. You're not locked into a one "true self" who never evolves.

My encouragement to you is to be self-aware, to know who you are and what you value. But then, as a leader, be aware of the other. Adopt a posture that will equip you to help other people move forward, to achieve key objectives and accomplish the goals you've set. It can be very individualistic—even selfish—to always focus on yourself and on how you are expressing yourself in the world instead of also thinking about the other people who have to receive it. You can often be more effective focusing less on authenticity and reflecting more on how people are responding to you as a leader. Is the "authentic" attitude you're using producing the results you desire?

If you're struggling to achieve the correct balance, let me share one last recommendation: Why not consider *alignment* rather than authenticity? Are the actions and behaviors and strategies you're using in alignment with both your values and your goals? If you're aspiring to a new role, why not test out different behaviors? Why not try biting your tongue instead of lashing out? Why not focus on different aspects of your role?

Behaviors may not feel natural; they may not feel like you at first. But certain behaviors may be required of specific roles and goals. As long as you're living in alignment with your values, you are still being true to your notion of self.

So, consider your answer to these questions: Am I living in alignment with the future I wish to create? What do I really want from this situation—for myself and for others? How would I behave if I really did want this? Answering these questions is perhaps the very best lens through which to view authenticity.

Who you are will certainly change, especially as you try new roles and new behaviors. What you value may change. But if, at each stage of your career, you pause to examine whether you are living in alignment with the future you wish to create—if your behaviors and attitudes are supporting and aligning with that future—then you are being authentic.

Reflection Points

1. Are your current behaviors inspiring your team?

   _____

   _____

   _____

   _____

   _____

2. Do your current behaviors support your drive to become the person you imagine yourself becoming?

   _____

   _____

   _____

   _____

3. Are you in alignment with the life you want to create?

_____

_____

_____

_____

_____

4. Are you willing to feel the discomfort of trying new things that may not immediately feel right in support of your goal of moving into leadership?

_____

_____

_____

_____

_____

CHAPTER TWELVE

EMBRACE THE NEUTRAL ZONE

Working out the fear of success, the fear of failure, and finally burning through to just pure activity.

–NATALIE GOLDBERG

I was thinking recently about birthdays—about my birthday, in fact—and the gap between what I imagine for the day and what I actually do with it. Kids love talking about their birthdays and planning parties and discussing who they want to invite, the type of cake they want to have, and the presents they'd like to receive. I used to be the same, spending hours, even days, planning for my birthday. But now, when my birthday is in my own hands, I don't own it. There is a gap between what I imagine for the day and what I do with it.

Birthdays may seem like frivolous stuff, but if you, like me, are not living the picture in your head on the more inane stuff, what does that mean for the rest of your life? For the big things? For the work you want to do, the network you want to build, the revenue you want to generate, the professional mark you want to leave? And for the art you want to immerse yourself in, the books you want to read, the relationships you want to rebuild, the journeys your heart longs for?

As you've read through this book, assessed the transitions you need to make, considered the tactics that you need to employ to equip yourself for leadership, you've created a new story. But only you can decide how and when to fully immerse yourself in this new narrative. Your future is literally in your own hands, but so many of us stay trapped between potential and practice—catching glimpses of who we are when we are in our power and articulating who we aspire to be yet remaining mired in a kind of ungrounded limbo, not living out this potential. Not putting it into practice.

I encourage many of the women I work with to "mind the gap." I want to share this same advice with you. Be careful of spiraling in this dark valley between potential and practice, as it leads to tremendous frustration and feelings of failure and despair.

You may be wrestling with some of these same doubts and feelings of discomfort. You begin, bright with promise and energy, vowing not to focus on perfection, determined to build new networks, resolving to become more strategic. But then you start to feel shaky and uncertain. As you start to say no to things in an effort to be more strategic, you may get rebuffed by others because of that no. You might reach out to other professionals to build new relationships and they may not respond. Or perhaps your pitch on a new direction is not well received. It's not going to feel great. And that's okay.

When you begin to take yourself up differently, when you test out new behaviors and perspectives, you may find yourself in an insecure position. The way you used to do things no longer fits, and yet your new environment, your new horizons, may seem alien and uncomfortable.

This is "the gap"—the messy middle between your old way of being, your old tendencies and associations, and the seemingly unreachable vision of who you would be. You no longer feel at home in your old way of doing things, yet you do not feel that you are fully embodying how you wish to behave and act and lead. You may even feel caught between the old way of how you saw yourself and the new possibilities of who you could be.

There is a reason why I've named these phases of career evolution as "transitions," not changes. Change is often more discreet. There's a beginning, a middle, and an end to it. You may have a new office, a new boss, a new policy to follow, or a new team to lead. In all of these changes, your focus is on the new thing, and your expectation is that, after a period of time, this change will end, the newness will become familiar.

Transition is different. Earlier I mentioned William Bridges and his influence on me with his work on transitions. His book *Managing Transitions: Making the Most of Change* laid much of the groundwork for my own philosophies on transitions. Most notably that the starting point for dealing with transition is not the outcome—the change itself—but the ending that you'll have to make to leave the old situation behind.

Transition begins with an ending—you have to say goodbye to a role or a behavior or a way of inhabiting your career that is no longer working. Something has stopped you from living the possibilities you want for yourself. Something is an obstacle to fully living into your passion. And a transition requires you to say goodbye to that thing, to let it go. It takes more time. And it usually is happening internally, in a way that may be invisible to others.

If you choose to move from perfection to passion, from clueless to connected, from being a worker bee to a strategic resource, you will need to say goodbye to the you who used to inhabit those roles. It's natural to feel regret and sadness that the tasks and roles that once brought meaning and purpose no longer do.

While you are in the neutral zone, the old way may be gone, but the new way is not yet fully operational. You haven't adapted yet; you may feel isolated and unproductive.

We spoke about pioneers at the start of this book. I'm sure that they, too, experienced this awkward, uncomfortable space between what was familiar and where they believed their true destination to be. There were certainly times when they were tempted to turn back, to return to what they knew. Many of them undoubtedly did.

You may feel these same temptations when you find yourself in the neutral zone. You may be tempted to go back to what feels comfortable and familiar. You may become stuck—clinging to what you know, afraid to advance any further. You may feel a sense of urgency to move ahead quickly, to advance to the next transition, before fully absorbing the lessons you need to learn.

As women, we sometimes try to create an artificial timeline: By the time I'm forty, I must be running my own company. By the time I'm fifty, I want to be on a board.

But you will have multiple careers, and each phase of your professional life will have its own rhythm. You show up, do the work every day, feel better, move forward, with each transition building on the next as your career evolves.

As you near the end of this book, it can be tempting to approach your career intellectually, with a set of boxes to tick and the "one right answer." The reality is that there is no single answer; life unfolds in interesting ways. At those points when you're tempted to wonder "Why is this happening to me?" instead ask "What is this teaching me?"

Navigating through the neutral zone is a necessary part of the process, but it is an interlude that marks a goodbye. There is an end point in your career that you have recognized, something that is no longer working.

Take your time to experience this ending. Understand that this ending must happen in order for you to take the next step in your story. You may need to begin to let go of a style of responding to others, an outlook on the world, a way of facing challenges.

My experience is that many of us misunderstand the cost of transitioning from old ways of doing things to new. We believe that, as this is often a transition of positive choice, it should go smoothly. If we have done the hard work of looking honestly at our professional lives and determining which paths we need to take to live a different future, the load should feel lighter. There should be new energy with each step forward.

But making the choice to change isn't easy.

And so, when we are brave enough to acknowledge that where we are now in our careers is incomplete, and then brave enough to articulate how we would begin to live our professional lives, moving toward a vision of self that inspires us, we expect good things supportive of this journey to flow toward us.

And when that does not happen automatically, we start to spiral. Bumps in the road start feeling like impassable obstacles. We seem incapable of learning from a few missteps and then correcting and moving forward. Instead of listening to our internal GPS and "recalculating" as we carry on, we feel as if we reel from one failure to another.

So how do you hold on to hope when you're in the neutral zone—hope that you are growing and changing in interesting ways? Hope that you are progressing toward the career you've envisioned. Hope that you may be embarking on the most fruitful and exciting period of your professional life.

Being in the neutral zone can leave you with questions as well as with a feeling of uncertainty. You don't yet know if these changes are working. You don't know whether or not you're successful.

CLIMBING THE SPIRAL STAIRCASE

My suggestion is to think about your answers to different questions. When you are in this kind of ungrounded limbo, consider what you have learned. What have you loved about this phase, when you felt like you were flip-flopping between that which was old and potentially easy and new ways of being and doing? What have you hated? What won't you forget? Even when you are in the neutral zone, there are times that are interesting, and there are opportunities for learning—for curiosity.

I also recommend creating some small places for certainty when you're feeling ungrounded. Simple rituals and daily practices can be quite helpful. Perhaps you want to build time into your day for meditation. Perhaps it's a long hot soak in a tub at the end of each day. Perhaps it's a morning walk or noontime snuggle with a baby. The secret is to not always focus on what's ahead, on looking forward, but instead on deciding how to live now, in this day.

> The secret is to not always focus on what's ahead, on looking forward, but instead on deciding how to live now, in this day.

As you move through a transition, you won't always be successful. If you're moving through the transition from perfection to passion, for example, you'll be successful in some areas, and in others you won't, and that can be shocking. People may reject you. You'll move forward and back in a series of stages.

It may help you to remember your leadership brand. To focus on the purpose of this transition. Pause for a moment and reflect on the value you bring and the attributes that make you unique.

I would like to close with what I regard as a quaint piece of Pittsburghese, my adopted hometown. Often, when there is a lull in conversation here, or to conclude a discussion, a local will say, "It is what it is." The expected response to that is: "Well, watcha gonna do about it?" Both of these statements are normally accompanied with a little sigh. They always struck me as terribly defeatist and borne of what this region has gone through in terms of boom-and-bust cycles.

But I have come to embrace the notion of "it is what it is." Things are what they are. So what? There is no perfect. There is no right or wrong way for you. There are mistakes and there are successes. There is enormous joy and deep sadness. There is regret and there are big dreams. Things are what they are. what they are.

> **As you move through a transition, you won't always be successful.**

But the question is, "Watcha gonna do about it?"

Whether it's planning your birthday or planning the next steps in your career, I encourage you to ask yourself that question: What will you do about it? Which next step will you take to navigate from where you are now to where you want to be?

It won't always feel comfortable. You will need to leave notions of perfect behind.

But every action, every small step, will move you forward.

Reflection Points

1. What needs to happen so that you can take the next step in your story?

_____

_____

_____

_____

_____

2. Which daily practice will you build into your day to keep you grounded during a transition?

_____

_____

_____

_____

_____

3. What are you learning during this season?

_____

_____

_____

_____

_____

THE SPIRALING STAIRCASE

My "bliss" has been the study of theology. For other people it may be a career in law or politics, a marriage, a love affair, or the raising of children. But that bliss provides us with the clue: If we follow it to the end it will take us to the heart of life.

—KAREN ARMSTRONG

When we are brave enough to acknowledge that where we are now in our career is not what we hoped, we can become brave enough to articulate how we can begin moving toward a professional vision that inspires us. The most helpful analogy I have found for what this process looks like comes from Karen Armstrong. She uses a spiral staircase to describe her "climb from darkness." The inspiration for this metaphor comes from T. S. Eliot's *Ash Wednesday*, a series of six poems that speak to the process of spiritual recovery. Eliot metaphorically climbs a spiral staircase in these poems, turning again and again to what he does not want to see as he slowly makes progress toward the light.

Far too many of us are doing this on our own, without role models. It's still relatively new, how women are being intentional about progressing in their careers and taking themselves up in a very serious way.

The women who are doing it successfully are very diverse. They've made different choices, and that diversity and difference have resulted in something very interesting.

In all of my exposure to different accounts of what it means to have a successful career or rich professional life, I have never found a story with a straight path. I truly have not seen overnight success. I have seen slow and steady and open eyes ready to learn and listen. I have seen many detours and hiccups along that path.

This process of closing the gap between potential and practice is about willingly turning, circling back over things we feel we may have already addressed—but each time with a new, higher understanding or consciousness. Each time we climb, always in an upward motion to heightened self-awareness and stronger understanding.

It's not about forcing insight.

At the same time, it's not about hiding in the shadows.

It is about taking that forward motion. Coming out from the shadows and climbing that spiral staircase. It won't always be easy, but ultimately, you will be okay.

In my own personal journey, initially my staircase was a straight-forward climb. I felt that my life, up to a point, had truly been one consistent success story. And it was only when I began to bring a real consciousness and truth to my professional life—choosing to immerse myself in the field of women's leadership development, building and then exiting an entrepreneurial venture, opting to move into an academic environment, streamlining a thriving coaching practice, etc.—that I started to fail miserably!

Here I was, making transitions of my own choosing, for the first time in many cases, and seemingly failing in a huge way. This rocked my confidence, especially as a mother of young children working outside the home in a foreign country with no familial support system. There were times I felt that I could not possibly think straight, or right, or for that matter see anything clearly at all.

My own judgment that I had always trusted seemed out of whack. Everyone else seemed to be providing feedback based more on where they were coming from instead of understanding where I was: in a very dark and lonely place. It was hard to find myself behind the hurts and the anger. Difficult to look at a life that took a different trajectory from what was imagined and anticipated.

Perhaps this resonates with your story. Perhaps you, too, are stuck in this weird place where you can't go back to who you were. It's too late. You can't ignore what you've discovered, and you are desperate to live and work differently, but the question is how. How do you move forward? How do you move toward that professional life you imagined?

One step on that spiraling staircase at a time.

Little steps or big ones. Know, with each step, each rotation, you are filling in the blanks on your résumé. Maybe you are learning to become a more mature adult—more nuanced, more compassionate. Perhaps you are building up internal reserves. Reclamation takes time. Slow and steady, regular practice, gaining mastery and then confidence and then flexing your muscles. That's what wins any race. Being able to stand in your world with grounded self-awareness and a clear sense of purpose, engaged in meaningful relationships, with depth, maturity, and perhaps more compassion for what you have seen and insight into what lies ahead.

As your career unfolds, as your life unfolds, you may find yourself circling back to a place you've been before. You may be at a point in your career where you are engaging in visionary behavior and then you pivot and discover that you're in a role that requires you to be more tactical and hands-on.

I love the spiral staircase as a metaphor for this experience because it truly is a metaphor for life. It may feel as if you are circling, revisiting different points before transitioning to others, but quietly, almost imperceptibly, you are evolving. You are moving forward—forward toward purpose.

That spiral staircase will lead you upward. And as you climb higher, you may need to pause and catch your breath. You may even need to step off for a while.

Too many of us expect their career to progress like an elevator. You jump on, push a button, and automatically advance to the next level. But that's not how a career works. That's not how life works.

That spiral staircase will lead you upward.

There are twists and turns. There are obstacles. There are new vistas and new discoveries.

It's not a straight path. But with each step, there is growth. There is learning. There is progress.

The staircase may seem daunting. Focus on taking just one step. If you don't try, if you don't begin to move, you will always wonder what might have been and who you might have become. Take that step and begin to move toward the professional life to which you've aspired.

MY OWN TRANSITION

At the beginning of this book, I talked about the importance of reclaiming your ambition. We shared our passion tokens and considered their symbolic importance as a method to regularly define and reflect on what matters.

This book reflects my own process of defining what matters and my own movement on that spiral staircase. It represents my transition toward the career I aspire to—one that creates a landscape where I can share new insights and deeper knowledge with the talented women like you who want to accelerate their careers.

I've recognized a desire to more fully immerse myself in doing work that is important to me and to have deeper conversations with women about how to strategically engage in the world. Like many of you, much of my career has unfolded around decisions impacting others. I've made pivots and taken on roles based on what my family needed, whether it was income, green cards, health insurance, or childcare.

I've experienced the M-shaped career and now find myself once more moving up and on, excited and energized by new opportunities to engage in work that is meaningful. I'm able to identify certain choices as safer and more comfortable and yet choose to step in a new direction, knowing that it has risks and may lead me into a place of uncertainty before I find my stride.

For me, the top of that spiral staircase holds my purpose, and it's toward this sense of purpose that I want to advance. I believe that my purpose includes you. It has been my mission for this book and for the next transition in my career: I want to help you figure things out. I want to help you navigate each stage of your career in a way that makes sense for your goals and your aspirations. I want you to recognize your sources of strength. Most of all, I want to join you in celebrating the unique twists and turns that have brought you to this place in your life.

YOUR STORY CONTINUES

This book may be coming to a close, but your story is just beginning. Throughout these chapters, we've talked very purposefully about career, about transitions and tactics. But let's take a breath for a moment. Let's acknowledge that your career will be long. It may involve several different careers, each with its own lessons, its own opportunities, its own transitions.

Let me lift any pressure you may be feeling to "get it right." You have time to figure it out. You are going to make mistakes, and it will be okay. You're going to move ahead and step back and circle around, just like the spiraling staircase.

My observation is that men's careers tend to be linear. They achieve in a linear way, moving steadily upward to a point where they retire and then give back to their family and their community. They shift their focus to relationships.

For women, it can be the absolute reverse. So many of us have taken time, in our careers, to contribute to our communities and to also care for family—for children, or siblings, or aging parents. You may still be in this stage, trying to "set the table" for what your career and your life will look like. Or you may be in a different stage, when you can now begin to focus on your career very differently.

There is great value in a rich and full life that includes work, family, and community, and there is tremendous encouragement in the knowledge that mature, seasoned women are in this way just beginning to hit their stride. It is a long runway; if you haven't yet made that first transition from perfection to passion, don't worry. There is still time.

Often, the women I coach come to me with specific goals in mind and a pressure to reach them quickly. They want to know how rapidly they can be promoted to VP, get on a board, or reach the C-suite.

But this singular focus on achievement—on roles and positions—in some ways can miss the mark. In addition, I encourage you to focus on your *impact*.

How many leaders have you developed—or will you develop? What innovations have you created and championed—and which will you create and champion? Which fresh ideas and visionary thinking have you contributed to your organization—and which are you nurturing today?

Throughout your life, you are leaving messages—for yourself and for the women who will follow. We are privileged to be living in an exciting time, when women are identifying and claiming and excelling in new ways, fully inhabiting careers that are rich with purpose and joy. And as members of this extraordinary group of women—

Throughout your life, you are leaving messages—for yourself and for the women who will follow.

these pioneers—our choices and actions create opportunities for those who are beside and behind us.

I don't want you to set down this book looking ahead to the next thing, and the next thing, and the next. I don't want you to be lost in this kind of transactional focus on roles. Instead, if you begin to assess your impact, the ways in which you have created value, you'll understand that the opportunities ahead are much broader than a role or a title.

I want you to look up. Look up to the places where you can begin to create work and a life of which you are proud. Look up to a life of purpose.

WORK WITH ME

Thank you for taking the time to explore the topics in this book further with me. If you're interested in continuing the conversation or even in working with me in the future, please reach out via Info@LeanneMeyer.com or visit my website at www.LeanneMeyer.com where you can learn more about my coaching and consulting services and how to book me for your upcoming keynotes, workshops, book clubs, or seminars.

In reading this book (and hopefully also sharing it with others!), you've officially become part of my dear community. If you'd like, feel free to connect with me and other community members via social media:

LinkedIn: www.linkedin.com/in/leannemeyer
Facebook: www.facebook.com/leanne.meyer.77
Instagram: www.instagram.com/leanne.m.meyer
Twitter: https://twitter.com/leanne_meyer

I look forward to staying in touch!

ABOUT THE AUTHOR

Leanne Meyer directs the Carnegie Mellon Women's Executive Leadership Academy at the Tepper School of Business and is the former executive director of the university's Accelerate Leadership Center.

Drawing from her thirty years of senior-level and executive development, she consults and coaches regularly. Her work focuses on assisting leaders in navigating critical inflection points where many have outgrown their professional identity and, given the demands and responsibility of their roles, need to change their perspectives regarding what is important and, accordingly, how they spend their time and what new skill sets and behaviors they develop. Her clients include a number of Fortune 100 large and midsize companies.

Leanne holds a master's degree in industrial psychology from the University of Johannesburg. Her calling is to help leaders make sense of their lives through the reclamation of passion and purpose.

Her career and creativity are anchored in leadership development—in helping people discover their potential, stand strong in their values, claim their worth, and believe in their talents to become the leaders they want to be in ways that embrace possibility and potential.

Beginning in South Africa, she's had the good fortune to follow this calling on three continents in corporate, academic, and not-for-profit settings, as business leader, program designer and developer, entrepreneur, facilitator, speaker, educator, and coach.